SEVEN STRATEGIES FOR POSITIVE AGING

A NORTON PROFESSIONAL BOOK

SEVEN STRATEGIES
FOR POSITIVE AGING

ROBERT D. HILL

W. W. Norton & Company
New York • London

For information about permission to reproduce selections from this book,
write to Permissions, W. W. Norton & Company, Inc., 500 Fifth Avenue,
New York, NY 10110

For information about special discounts for bulk purchases,
please contact W. W. Norton Special Sales at specialsales@wwnorton.com or
800-233-4830

Manufacturing by Haddon Craftsmen
Production manager: Leeann Graham

Library of Congress Cataloging-in-Publication Data

Hill, Robert D.
Seven strategies for positive aging / Robert D. Hill. — 1st ed.
p. cm. — (A Norton professional book)
Practical exercises and information in a workbook complement to
Positive Aging.
Includes bibliographical references and index.
ISBN 978-0-393-70523-2 (pbk.)
1. Gerontology. 2. Older people—Health and hygiene. 3. Quality of life.
I. Hill, Robert D. Positive aging. II. Title.
HQ1061. H534 2008
305.26—dc22
2007040497

W. W. Notron & Company, Inc., 500 Fifth Avenue,
New York, N.Y. 10110
www.wwnorton.com

W. W. Norton & Company Ltd., Castle House,
75/76 Wells Street, London W1T 3QT

1 3 5 7 9 0 8 6 4 2

I express appreciation to my wife and life companion, Debra K. Hill,
for her assistance in the preparation and editing of this book,
and to my mother, Betty Hill Badasci, for her support.

CONTENTS

INTRODUCTION

The opening of the 21st century has yielded revolutionary pathways to physical and psychological health. Championed by the Positive Psychology movement (Seligman & Csikszentmihalyi, 2000), we now have permission to choose life satisfaction and well-being as markers of health regardless of our physical condition. Through processes embedded in valued subjective experience we have learned that disciplining how we think and feel about ourselves and our health is as important to well-being as any physiological markers of disease. The field of positive psychology has transformed our understanding of the power of the mind to influence life satisfaction. It is from this backdrop that the term *Positive Aging* has emerged. Positive Aging describes a process whereby we take control of our own late life experience by discovering meaning in growing old that transcends the deteriorative processes of aging.

In my previous book, *Positive Aging: A Guide for Mental Health Professionals and Consumers* (Hill, 2005), I defined "Positive Agers" as possessing four characteristics. These, I asserted, are powerful sources of coping with our vulnerabilities that arise as we grow old. These characteristics are: (a) mobilizing resources to meet the challenges of aging, (b) making life choices that preserve well-being, (c) cultivating flexibility to deal with age-related decline, and (d) focusing on the positives (versus the negatives) in old age. Positive Aging characteristics have been elucidated by the science of gerontology as attributes of people who have figured out how to live life well and derive meaning from engaging in self-improvement as well as promoting growth in others. They are concepts that are part of nearly every theory of adult life-span development and are the building blocks of maturity in old age.

I refer to *maturity* in the context of Positive Aging to describe the adaptive potential that comes from the interplay between your unique character and personal attributes and how you use these to manage your living environment. We all know that our living situation and personal circumstances will change as we age, and this can challenge our sense of who we are and how we relate to the world.

Transitions that could occur as a consequence of aging might include learning to live alone when your partner or spouse passes away, downsizing your residence so that you can manage domestic tasks on your own, or moving out of your home and into an assisted living facility (or a younger family member's home) when you are no longer able to take care of yourself without help. Maturity is making these kinds of transitions and preserving your sense of dignity and happiness in the process.

Theorists of adult development and aging have described maturation as the interaction between our environment and our nature and how this interplay influences who we are and how we think about ourselves in relation to others. Erik Erikson, a pioneer in adult life-span development who defined the life span as a series of eight stages, labeled the final two stages as *generativity versus self-absorption* and *integrity versus despair* (Erikson, Erikson, & Kivnick, 1986). Erikson asserted that we continue to develop ourselves (and mature) in adulthood as we grow from experience and adapt to our world. "Generativity" means promoting growth in others who are younger and "integrity" means grounding your behavior in a stable framework of values and beliefs. In Erikson's own words:

> In each developmental stage, the individual thus experiences a creative tension between the two opposites, a tension that attracts both instinctive and instinctual energy . . . which thus provide, even as they depend on, individual development (p. 39).

Erikson's belief was that "individual development" results from extracting benefits from experiences to address the difficulties and challenges in life and in old age (Erikson, Erikson, & Kivnick, 1986).

Maintaining our integrity and gaining maturity is an essential tenant in Positive Aging. This idea was captured by Robert Atchley (1999), a contemporary life-span theorist, who proposed that maturity is a form of continuity or a propensity for stability across the life span. Atchley provided evidence of how developmental continuity works, in stories and data that he presented from the "Ohio Long-Term Care Research Project." Here, he juxtaposed our propensity to maintain stability in how we think, feel, and relate to the world while at the same time adapting to the forces of change that are inherent in aging. His case study of Edna illustrated this dynamic:

> By 1991, Edna's physical mobility problems had worsened considerably, but at age 88 she still maintained her very positive outlook on life. . . . She adapted her lifestyle to her more homebound state by doing less gardening and cutting back on her participation in politics. . . . However, she . . . spent more time with her collection of family photographs and memorabilia, and watched more television. . . . Adapting to her changing mobility was a major goal . . . and she accomplished this goal with her usual positive approach, planning, and creativity. In 1995, Edna still had very high morale, a realistic appraisal of her personal agency and a very . . . satisfying life. (pp. 19–20)

Edna, in the face of change, cultivated the fourth characteristic of Positive Aging: "focusing on the positives in old age." For her, it was easy to be positive even in pain because this was her nature. She had acquired a lifestyle pattern of "valuing the positives" and used this characteristic as she encountered challenges associated with growing old that might cause others to despair. In her view, why not take the positive approach, even though her mobility was being permanently restricted as a result of age-related decline? To focus on the negatives would, for Edna, be a recipe for discouragement and prevent her from realizing her goals.

How did Edna acquire this Positive Aging characteristic? Was it a trait that she was born with? Did someone teach her at an earlier impressionable time in her life how to "find the positives in living," which she then practiced as she grew older? Perhaps she discovered this approach as she was struggling with a particular life challenge. Not only are we left to wonder "how" Edna developed this remarkable quality, but the question about whether we can develop this kind of Positive Aging characteristic ourselves remains.

It is the assertion of this book that the characteristics of Positive Aging come from practicing strategies that promote optimal adjustment in old age. I have identified seven that are supported by data from the science of gerontology to help you get the most out of late-life living. I have phrased these strategies as an admonition to send the message that it is not only possible, through following them, to find happiness in later life, but that they can be acquired by everyone.

THE SEVEN STRATEGIES FOR POSITIVE AGING

- You can find meaning in old age.
- You're never too old to learn.
- You can use the past to cultivate wisdom.
- You can strengthen life-span relationships.
- You can promote growth through giving and receiving help.
- You can forgive yourself and others.
- You can possess a grateful attitude.

These seven strategies for Positive Aging embody an approach to living that has been found in a variety of contexts and across a range of people to mobilize resources for well-being in later life. These strategies can be learned by anyone and, if mastered, will nurture an affirmative approach to living and produce the attributes you need to adapt to some of the most difficult challenges that life can deal out. A basic assumption behind each of the seven strategies is that from them come concrete activities that people can engage in to enhance meaning in life. There are no prerequisites for learning these strategies and they work for people of all races, cultures, and lifestyle practices. Your personal resources do not dictate whether you can know and practice these strategies, so you will find individuals who are proficient in using them who are either healthy or sick, rich or poor, literate or illiterate, white or black, and young or old.

This book provides guidelines for incorporating these strategies into your daily lifestyle. Each chapter corresponds to a specific strategy. I have summarized these below:

Chapter 1, "You Can Find Meaning in Old Age," describes how generating meaning in later life fits with Positive Aging. In this chapter a framework for coping with old age is introduced. This framework comes from the science of adult life-span development, which teaches that life unfolds as a series of phases or stages in which we find different sources of meaning. Meaning comes from our evolving interests, our occupations, our social circles, and our values and beliefs. A fulfilling life is one that has meaning and Positive Agers are meaning finders. One of the greater fears in growing old is loss of meaning, especially as we experience the death of loved ones, changes in our living circumstances, and age-related memory decline. In Positive Aging, however, meaning is found even in loss and decline. Several techniques for meaning generation in these circumstances are examined: (a) reframing decline as an opportunity to focus on the things that are really important in life while at the same time letting go of those things of less value, (b) making life choices that help you continue to find meaning, (c) strategies for the preservation of functioning in old age including a behavioral coping technique known as SOC (selectivity, optimization, and compensation), and (d) learning how to reframe challenges as opportunities for personal growth.

Chapter 2, "You're Never Too Old to Learn," describes how engaging in lifelong learning preserves intellect in old age. Learning keeps active those tendencies that help us to stay youthful in how we think and feel. Curiosity, the pursuit of knowledge just for the fun of it, and discovery, and the role of self-reflection as a form of personal renewal, are important elements in lifelong learning. A Positive Aging approach to learning involves finding new resources to awaken dormant capacities that can be applied to enhance your ability to learn in your later years. This chapter tackles the issue of cognitive problems and how learning can be a source of Positive Aging even in diseases of aging like Alzheimer's.

Chapter 3, "You Can Use the Past to Cultivate Wisdom," describes developing Positive Aging skills to enhance maturation in old age. The full expression of maturation in later life is wisdom. People are not wise just because they are old. This chapter asserts that wisdom comes in later life only to the extent that we learn from our past to make our present and future better. The first part of this chapter describes a framework from the adult life-span literature through which wisdom emerges, namely, continuity theory. This theory describes how the stability of our nature unfolds as we age. Strategies for maintaining stability in later life, while at the same time retaining our capacity for change by learning from the past, are described. You will explore your tolerance for change and how you can use what you know and who you are to improve your present and future circumstances. Finally, you will learn how, through Positive Aging skills, you can make life choices that preserve your well-being and allow you to teach others how to find life satisfaction in the process.

Chapter 4, "You Can Strengthen Life-span Relationships," describes how maintaining and enhancing meaningful relationships in old age cultivates Positive Aging. We all belong to a social network or a convoy of relationships. Our role in this social convoy comes from the frequency and the quality of interchange we have with others. This involves a triad of belonging behaviors: interaction-concern-caring. The role that these belonging behaviors play in helping you to address relationship issues in the course of aging, including dealing with loneliness and loss, is explored. The skill of belonging can help you to manage your social network and is an important Positive Aging resource.

Chapter 5, "You Can Promote Growth Through Giving and Receiving Help," describes how cultivating altruism through acts of helping can promote Positive Aging. Helping involves both giving and receiving assistance and the science of gerontology has identified giving help and volunteerism as sources of physical renewal and enhanced longevity in old age. This chapter presents the principles of help giving that promote Positive Aging. Help receiving and how you can be an instrument for promoting growth in others by knowing how to receive help graciously is also described.

Chapter 6, "You Can Forgive Yourself and Others," describes how you can engender forgiveness in your later years. Forgiveness involves forgiving others, yourself, and circumstances. The nature and concept of forgiveness as a pathway to better health are reviewed. Emotions such as kindness, compassion, and sympathy emerge as one develops a forgiving approach to living. It is the recognition that the world is not perfect and that forgiveness is needed to repair damage and hurt that makes you a Positive Ager. This chapter explores why both the giving and the receiving of forgiveness are part of Positive Aging. Forgiveness steps and how you can apply these steps to overcome hatred and animosity are described. The role of forgiveness in dealing with past grievances is addressed.

Chapter 7, "You Can Possess a Grateful Attitude," describes how being grateful promotes Positive Aging. Gratitude is a powerful reframing strategy that allows you to take challenges and difficulties and make them into opportunities for personal development. Employing gratitude to deal with the vicissitudes of old age is described. There are specific skills one develops over the course of life that facilitate the ability to feel grateful. Gratitude is presented as a way of dealing with difficult emotions associated with late-life transitions, to address loss, and to help you find the positives in old age.

WHO IS THIS BOOK FOR?

Seven Strategies for Positive Aging is for every person who wants to get the most out of later life. It is also for the person who is dissatisfied with the prospect of becoming inactive and discarded in old age. If you are in an age transition such as retiring from your employment, caring for an impaired loved one, relocating because of age-related disability, or grieving the loss of a loved one, the principles of Positive Aging can help you find meaning in the process. How you deal with life is a product of who you are, the living skills you acquire along the way, and how you apply those skills in coping with the challenges of growing old. Positive Aging will help you discover new ways to refine your existing abilities so that you can discover meaning and happiness in your later years.

SEVEN STRATEGIES FOR POSITIVE AGING

Chapter 1

STRATEGY #1: YOU CAN FIND MEANING IN OLD AGE

I. MEANING IN OLD AGE

If you are living in your sixth decade or beyond, you have faced the reality that you are old and, as average life expectancy approaches the eighth decade, you will spend an appreciable portion of your life as a "Senior Citizen." This powerful statistic raises new issues about what it means to grow old. The pressing question on the minds of today's generation of adults is no longer "How long will I live?" but "If I'm going to live such a long time, how can I be happy in the process?" To be sure, poll after poll tells us that what most people fear about growing old is loss. When a recent *USA Today* survey of 1,000 adults (ages 18–80 years) posed the question "What concerns you the most about growing old?" top responses were: (a) losing my health (73%) and (b) losing the ability to take care of myself (70%) (Manning, 2005).

In late life we lose our youthful looks, our health declines, and our stamina fades. There is no escaping the physical vulnerability and functional loss that are associated with advancing age. We fear aging because it represents a widening "gap" between what we are able to do and what we want to do. This is known as functional loss.

When you are young and in good health, you give little thought to functional loss because your abilities and the demands that are part of your everyday living are in balance. As you grow old, however, this balance is disrupted as it becomes more difficult to accomplish your daily routines. Most people worry about functional loss not only in activities such as washing the dishes, making the bed, or keeping finances in order, but also for basic self-care tasks like feeding yourself, dressing yourself, and getting out of your bed in the morning. When self-care activities start to be affected by loss, then there is a substantial press for you to need help from another person or even to move from your home or independent living residence into a facility where you can get this help on an ongoing basis. This is what is at the root of the *USA Today* poll quoted earlier. The real fear of old age is that for most people it means functional loss.

The science of gerontology is engaged in an all-out effort to understand the phenomenology of loss and the role it plays as a consequence of extended longevity. Some compelling research in this area comes from the Boston Longitudinal Study of Normal Aging (BLSA) (Shock et al., 1984). The BLSA is famous for highlighting three themes that fit the paradigm of loss in old age termed "age-related decline."

The first theme is that age-related decline is distinct from decline due to disease. This difference is not only in the slope of the trajectory of decline (decline is steeper when disease is present), but also in the variability of decline between individuals. A manifestation of this is that in age-related decline when disease is not present, some 70-year-olds seem like they are 50 years old, whereas other 70-year-olds seem like they are 90 years old. This is not necessarily the case when disease is present. In disease, the rate of decline becomes more predictable and follows a severity trajectory. Whether you are young or old, the greater the severity of your illnesses, the steeper your rate of decline. Figure 1.1 depicts the differences in these trajectories. In this figure you can see that chronological age runs along the horizontal axis and the rate of decline runs along the vertical axis. Three facts can be taken from this figure to understand how age-related decline impacts late-life functioning: (a) In normal aging people live longer than those who are aging in the presence of disease. Therefore, in normal aging you will experience less decline in older age than in diseased aging. (b) The rate of decline is steeper when disease is present. This means that your functional deficits will appear more abruptly than in normal aging, where the process of

2

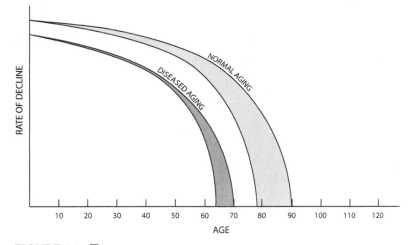

FIGURE 1.1. TRAJECTORIES OF NORMAL AND DISEASED AGING.

decline is more subtle and may occur over a longer time period. (c) The range of age when a person dies is wider for those who are aging in the absence of disease. Figure 1.1 also underscores the point that when you are sick, you die sooner and the age range will be narrow because, presumably, the disease—not aging—is in control of your trajectory of decline. This is why doctors can pinpoint time of death more accurately in a person who has disease than in a person who is disease free.

The second theme from the BLSA studies is that there are specific consequences of age-related decline. For example, almost everyone who grows old experiences some form of memory impairment. However, other mental processes, such as the ability to use words or remember facts from history, are often preserved in old age. Sometimes these differences in how abilities are affected by age-related decline can be quite troublesome. You may be feeling very healthy and mentally intact, but when you encounter a task that puts pressure on those abilities that are sensitive to age-related decline, such as remembering a name or quickly coming up with a specific word, you will be confronted with this age-related deficit as it affects your day-to-day living. At first, a memory problem is only annoying, but it can become troublesome even if it is not an emerging disease process. Since "who you are" is a product of "what you can remember," loss of memory can create a fear of loss of meaning as you get older.

The third theme is an extension of the old adage that "no one is getting out of here alive." Now there is a new idiom: "No one is getting out of here without encountering age-related decline." It doesn't matter how healthy you are or how well you take care of yourself; if you live long enough you will experience loss due to age-related decline, and if you live into very old age you will likely need help to perform even the most common activities that you do now without even thinking about it: brushing your teeth, combing your hair, using the toilet, eating a meal.

Among the 72,000 individuals who are centenarians (those living to be 100 years and older) in the United States, most live in residential care facilities or protected environments because their advanced age has impaired their functioning to such a degree that they are highly vulnerable to accidents, health problems, and death. If you are lucky enough to live to be 100, you will be unlucky as well because your ability to engage in the everyday tasks will be compromised to the point that you will need help to get along in life.

There is a pattern in loss that I have termed the "four Ds of decline": dysfunction, disability, dependency, and death. These "four Ds" underscore how decline will affect you and influence your life satisfaction and well-being. The meaning of each of the "four Ds of decline" is below.

• Dysfunction: When you experience dysfunction, you can still perform everyday tasks, but these become more difficult and you will need to take more time or develop alternative strategies to function at the same level that you did when you did not have dysfunction. You may still be able to open a tight lid, but your muscle strength may have diminished so that it is easier to use a lid opener that gives you a bit more leverage to perform the task.

• Disability: Disability means that you can no longer perform a task by yourself, even using alternative strategies, so you must get help to perform it. In this case, you may not be able to open the tight jar lid even with the lid opener, so you need to call a neighbor to help you open the lid. Experiencing disability does not mean that you are dependent—many disabled older adults function independently; however, you must have help to perform tasks associated with everyday living, especially tasks that involve household chores and getting goods and services from your community. Many disabled people can engage in self-care such as bathing, toileting, feeding, dressing, and transporting themselves around the house using creative strategies to assist them. If you can comb your hair, brush your teeth, eat your meals, and get out of bed, but you can't drive a car, balance your checkbook, or iron your clothes, you are disabled, but you are not necessarily dependent.

• Dependency: Dependency means that you cannot function on your own nor can you care for yourself without help. Critical in dependency is that you need help to perform some of the simple self-care activities such as brushing your teeth, eating your meals, getting out of bed, and using the toilet. If you can't perform these tasks without help, or have difficulty doing them even with help, then you are dependent.

• Death: Death is the end state of decline. It is a stage in the process of decline where all functioning comes to an end. It involves a special aspect of decline where you cease to function and it is likely that prior to that cessation in old age, there is substantial diminishment of your functional abilities, including your mental and physical health. Some researchers have identified a phenomenon known as "terminal drop," which is when all of your functions take a final jump downward just prior to your death.

There are two common themes across these "Ds." First, they are almost always encountered in the order listed above. Second, although the science of aging is finding ways to slow their progression, the pathway through these four stages of aging is unavoidable.

It is important to note here that *Disease* starts with a D, but I have not included it as one of the "four Ds" because it is not necessary for disease to be present for decline to occur. Disease, as discussed, may affect decline, but not everyone who is old is afflicted by disease. In fact, the science of gerontology has coined the term *frailty* (Hamerman, 1999) to describe decline that is not connected to an illness or a disease. Frailty acknowledges the fact that as you get old you will have fewer and fewer resources to function normally, and your risk for experiencing problems with everyday living will become greater as you age. Being frail does not mean that you are weak or unable or that you have an unhealthy lifestyle; it simply means that you are declining (Verbrugge and Jette, 1994).

In a society where most people don't want to grow old and fear frailty, the psychological impact of the "four Ds" on your potential well-being should not be underestimated. Decline can usher in a personal crisis of meaning in old age. This is captured in a quote from the late well-known *New Yorker* writer Malcolm Cowley (1980) who described his own experience of living into his ninth decade and the emergent realization of his own aging:

> The new octogenarian [Cowley had just had his 80th birthday] feels as strong as ever when he is sitting back in a comfortable chair. He ruminates, he dreams, he remembers. He doesn't want to be disturbed by others. It seems to him that old age is only a costume assumed for those others; the true, the essential self is ageless. In a moment he will rise and go for a ramble in the woods. . . . Then he creaks to his feet, bending forward to keep his balance, and realizes that he will do nothing of the sort. The body and its surroundings have their messages for him, or only one message: "You are old." (p. 3)

Cowley's words reveal how the "four Ds" can affect you as you age.

There is, however, another fear in Cowley's story that is less obvious, but perhaps as important: the fear that comes from the messages that society gives to you as an older person, which is, "You are old." When you are old, society expects you to act your age. Older people are sick, older people are ugly, older people are obsolete, and older people are definitely not sexy. Even in the 21st century, these messages persist, and they become more pronounced as you live beyond your eighth decade, since some features of physical appearance are simply unable to stay healthy and youthful-looking no matter what effort you make to offset the wear and tear of aging. There is no surgery, no special form of exercise, no cream, no drug that will return a 95-year-old's skin into the supple, smooth skin of a baby. It is nearly impossible to return the tone in your muscles at 70 years of age to what it was when you were in your 20s. The manifestations of age-related decline will affect what you do and how you feel about your own aging experience.

I have now established that as you age you decline; however, Positive Agers don't need to feel that they are less of a person or that their needs should be dismissed or that they aren't entitled to life satisfaction and well-being just because they are old.

Surely, there must be more optimistic ways of thinking about our own aging that gives us permission to shed our fears and find pathways to happiness in being old even as natural changes in our physical condition and enduring social stereotypes press on our awareness. Is it possible to experience age-related decline in a way that does not rob us of the ability to feel good about living and anticipating our future as we age?

Positive Aging makes no claim that it will forestall the "four Ds of decline." It does offer an alternative way for you to think and feel about growing old, helping you find meaning in the process. In fact, Positive Aging is a viewpoint that asserts that meaning is as strong in the twilight of life as it is at any other time.

II. POSITIVE AGING: OLD AGE AS A SOURCE OF MEANING

Positive Aging involves adopting an affirmative mind-set that not only acknowledges decline as a natural process of growing old, but emphasizes its advantages as a source of finding meaning in old age. For example, we can think narrowly about decline as loss, or we can view it as an element of broader life-span characteristics that are at the center of how we find personal meaning. Most people mature as they age, and maturation in later life produces qualities such as insight, astuteness, common sense, shrewdness, sagacity, and wisdom.

As you progress through life you are expected to grow up, or mature. Those who care about you, including your parents, grandparents, teachers, and friends, may encourage you to have experiences that help you mature. Maturation is aided in youth by such activities as going away to college with the hope that you will develop new skills to meet life's challenges. Other events, such as marriage, your first job, moving away from your home of origin, or military service, are all experiences that can help you mature. Maturation as a kind of age-related change is viewed uniformly in youth as a force for good. Aging does not necessarily ensure maturity, but those people who make the most contributions in life—to their own self-development and to the development of others—have acquired capacities through maturation.

Positive Aging asserts that maturation continues into old age and those who mature cultivate personal characteristics that help them refine their ability to find satisfaction in living and cope with its challenges. Maturity in later life may not manifest itself in the same way as it does in youth. In youth, maturation emerges as one acquires new skills and abilities. In old age, maturation involves applying existing abilities and skills to address challenges, including those due to age-related decline. In both cases, the concept of maturation presumes that you become better over time at addressing the issues of life, whether learning new skills or adapting to functional loss. They both involve refining yourself in the process.

Begley (2007) proposed that there are positive aspects of brain aging due to maturational processes. For example, research on how older professionals benefit from the strategic access to information, based on their many years of dealing with problems in their profession, facilitates solution finding. Begley (2007) states,

> older professionals can readily separate what's important from what's not, a big reason so many of them fire on all cognitive cylinders well past age 65. 'In complex business litigation, [says Mark Zauderer, 60, a partner in the New York law firm Flemming, Zulack, Williason Zuderer], a lawyer must be able to sort the wheat from the chaff. A senior lawyer is in the best position to do that, and to have the courage to discard facts—even those on your side—that will only distract the court or the jury.'

Begley also describes how brain aging can mediate negative emotional states. She states that the important point is that there is emerging data that argues for the phenomenon of "brain maturity" that not only compensates for age-related decline but may also improve coping with everyday functions in later life.

Older adults who are Positive Agers learn how to change and adapt to living and in the process feel better about their own aging, even though this may mean that they no longer have the capacities and capabilities that they had in youth.

A metaphor that is useful in understanding the concept of maturational processes in age-related decline is what many people experience when, in their later years, they attend their high school or college reunion. Reunions are meaningful social events and they are popular because, among other things, they provide people with a sense of age-group continuity. Of interest here is the role that the reunion plays in reminding people of what it means to live in the presence of age-related decline as shown in the story below.

> Steve attended his 50-year high school reunion. In describing this experience he was impressed by the changes in the physical characteristics of his classmates. Many were not nearly as attractive as he once remembered them being in high school and a number detailed health problems, such as cancer and heart disease. A few were overweight and some complained of failing memory. The most popular girls in high school were now middle-aged women whose beauty had weathered over time. There were, interestingly, several of his classmates who had aged remarkably well. In fact, they almost seemed to have improved over time. Yes, they were older, but they portrayed a sense of health, energy for living, and vitality that several of them did not possess when they were younger. These classmates had seemed to "find themselves." Steve wondered why aging had favored these classmates and not the others. He enjoyed this reunion more than previous ones because he discovered some common events that he and his classmates had experienced across their lives.

This reunion story illustrates the obvious fact about the "four Ds" in that "the longer you live the more you decline." However, less obvious in this vignette is the fact that some people adapted to old age and actually got better in some areas of living. Those who had adapted well seemed to experience preservation of their vitality in later life even in the presence of age-related decline. This does not mean that these people were slowing or reversing their own aging. On the contrary, they were applying the strategies of Positive Aging by focusing on their assets as a source of meaning rather than their deficits. They found ways to be happy and feel vital even when confronting decline.

Positive Aging is not how to avoid, dodge, or even suspend age-related decline and its deficits, but rather to understand it, learn how to live with it, and deal with its effects, even to reframe decline not as loss, but rather as a source of meaning that can make being old worthwhile. The four characteristics of Positive Aging represent guiding principles to help you transform the process of aging and age-related decline:

- Mobilizing Resources
- Making Affirmative Life Choices
- Cultivating Flexibility
- Focusing on the Positives

Mobilizing Resources

To find resources to cope with age-related decline, consider the meaning of the "four Ds." If you can suspend your worry about them as a marker of loss, you can reframe them as indicators that you need to mobilize personal coping resources. Obviously, decline indicates that your resources are diminishing, but it also tells you about the capacities that you have left. So if your goal is to mobilize your resources, Positive Aging is to think of the resources that you have—and how to use them. Aging in this sense involves an interaction between your changing capabilities, the nature of the task itself, and how you have engaged in the task in the past. For example, if age-related decline in your vision has made reading the newspaper more difficult, then you are best served not to simply give up on reading and become distressed over this loss, but assess what vision you have left and use it in a way that allows you to continue to read. You might buy a magnifying glass or reading glasses to enlarge the print so you can continue to read the newspaper. It may be that your remaining eyesight will last for a very long time, and reading with the magnifying glass can allow you to continue this activity and get satisfaction from it. In fact, you might obtain some new skills in the process of reading with magnification, such as improved attention to picture detail, that will provide you with new information that the typical reader might not attend to.

In this example, you are not afraid of your declining functioning, but you are acknowledging that it exists. Then, given that this deficit in vision is present, you are mobilizing resources by finding a way to compensate for the deficit and continue functioning. To do this, you must approach the task differently than you did before in order to preserve your ability to continue reading. You are mobilizing your resources and finding new meaning in aging by changing not only how you view the task, but also your behaviors, so that reading remains doable and enjoyable in the presence of age-related deficits.

The science of life-span adaptation has expanded our understanding about how Positive Agers recruit resources to alter age-related deficits. At the Max Planck Institute in Germany scholars in adult development and aging have proposed a cultural-behavioral classification system that they believe Positive Agers employ to cope with decline. This system is labeled SOC, which is an acronym for "selectivity, optimization, and compensation" (Baltes, 1997). Older adults who are better at adapting to age-related decline use SOC in the following ways: They first make strategic discriminations to limit their options in order to remain functional even as their faculties decline (selectivity). Next, they identify skills that are essential for preserving quality of life in old age and they practice those skills (optimization). Finally, after limiting options or practicing essential skills becomes insufficient to preserve functioning, a Positive Ager gets assistance from the external environment, i.e. buying a cane to facilitate walking even when one's physical capacity for maintaining balance during mobility is impaired (compensation). In the reading example already mentioned, obtaining a tool to increase magnification either in the form of a magnifying glass or reading glasses is an example of compensation.

Baltes, Staudinger, and Undenberger (1999) provided an example of how adaptation to age-related deficits involves the interaction of these processes in a highly skilled task; namely, playing the piano:

> When the concert pianist Arthur Rubinstein, as an 80-year-old, was asked in a television interview how he managed to maintain such a high level of expert piano playing, he hinted. . . . First, he played fewer pieces (selection); he practiced these pieces more often (optimization); and to counteract his loss in mechanical speed he now used a kind of impression management, such as playing more slowly before fast segments to make the latter appear faster (compensation). (pp. 483–484)

Rubenstein adapted his functioning by selecting fewer pieces that were the most meaningful to perform (selectivity). Although having a larger range of pieces available adds variety and spontaneity to a performance, the ability to play proficiently was a desirable trade-off.

Once he had determined his limited repertoire, he practiced these to offset lapses that might occur in his memory, motor processes, or attention (optimization). Finally, he engaged in some performance alterations by slowing the tempo of some portions of the score to accentuate the fluctuations in tempo necessary to fully perform a dynamic piece (compensation).

It is important to emphasize that SOC does not reverse age-related decline. Instead, SOC is a strategy for managing your changing capacities as you age so that you can continue to find well-being and satisfaction in your later years. Proficiency in using SOC cultivates qualities in later life that help you cope with its challenges and mature in the process. SOC users, like Rubenstein, would be considered mature, and maturity is obtained by the effort put forth to use SOC to address age-related decline.

The application of SOC, whether to maintain a skill, sustain oneself in the presence of a chronic age-related disablement, or recover from a setback due to aging, is an essential mechanism for preserving well-being in old age and very old age. It is a powerful Positive Aging example of how you can mobilize resources to address decline.

Making Affirmative Life Choices

How would you apply Positive Aging to deal with a deficit that is irretrievable? Take, for instance, your youthful appearance. If you are 50 or older and look in the mirror, you will notice that your young appearance has deteriorated. Your skin is particularly vulnerable to the effects of aging; it is likely to show wrinkles and perhaps even some discoloration. Your hair, as well, tends to be a physical marker of aging due to diminished pigmentation in the hair follicles. Convincing evidence that you are physically aging comes when you compare how you looked when you were young, say 20 years of age, to how you look when you are 50 or older. Contrasting current and past photographs of yourself will reveal dramatic differences in your appearance due to aging. There is not much that can be done to change the impact of age on your appearance. Even so, a plethora of strategies exists—skin creams and other commercial products, vitamins, and even plastic surgery—for those who want to try. For some, these alternatives may be meaningful.

However, to accept age-related change in appearance is to make a life choice that allows you to let go of the need to be youthful. Why not adopt a new life pattern that affirms your aging appearance? The selection of clothes or the choice of social relationships that do not place a high premium on looking young could be a powerful life choice that will free you from the longing to return to youth. Why worry about being youthful? It may be that being young is not even interesting anymore.

You can also think about your appearance and the nature of age-related deficits associated with your looks at a deeper level. Why do you want to look youthful? Do you connect youth to being physically attractive? It may be that underneath all of this is really your desire to feel good about yourself. If feeling good about yourself is the real goal, then a life choice of chasing the illusion of youthful appearance may not achieve your objective even if you were able to recapture youth. What are life choices that can help you feel good about yourself irrespective of your age? Several well-known lifestyle habits have been found to improve your sense of self-worth, whether you are 20 or 80 years old, such as

- Exercise.
- Eating the right foods.
- Stress relief.
- Trying new things.

These types of life choices can help improve your sense of self-worth regardless of age. The story below highlights this:

KAREN AND HER WEIGHT

Karen, a mother of four, had a weight problem for most of her adult life. She believed, at a relatively young age, that she needed to "watch her weight" because both of her parents were severely obese and her mother had tried for years unsuccessfully to lose weight. When Karen's mother, at age 67, developed pancreatic cancer, she became unable to eat and lost over 200 lbs prior to her death. Karen was very sad when her mother died; however, she believed that her mother did take on a new beauty in her illness because Karen had never seen her mother thin prior to the cancer. Karen married young and was eager to have a large family. At each childbirth, however, Karen became heavier and heavier, until after the fourth child Karen weighed nearly 280 lbs. For Karen, her weight was an emotional burden and a health problem; however, dieting, exercise, and medication were not effective in helping her to lose weight. Because she was so heavy, it was difficult for her to engage in exercise and to even walk up and down stairs. She felt that her weight was adversely affecting her marriage and she was very reluctant to engage in sexual relationships with her husband, Mike, because, as Karen noted, "When I look at myself in the mirror I wonder how anyone would want to have sex with me." Though she was overweight, she had an attractive face and long brown hair, and she had even been approached by an advertising agency to model plus-size clothing. After years of agonizing over her situation, she convinced her family that gastric bypass surgery was the only way she would be free of her weight problem. She identified a board-certified surgeon and began preparing for this surgery, which involved extensive individual and couples counseling. Her surgery was successful and she lost 150 lbs over the course of her surgery and recovery. She was determined to keep her weight off so she made lifestyle changes, including exercising daily and eating nutritiously. Over the course of several years, Karen was happier and healthier. I ran into Karen when she was 49 years old. I asked her how she was doing. She indicated that some things had actually improved with age. "When I was younger and overweight I struggled with sex, but now, even though my hair is gray and my skin is not as soft and smooth as it used to be, I enjoy sex more—in fact I've started initiating it, because I feel good about myself. Although people say that sex is better when you are younger, my experience is just the opposite. Sex is better now that I'm older. When it comes to sex, feeling good about myself trumps being younger."

For Karen, feeling good about herself was more important in a sexual relationship than being youthful. Although at 28 years of age she was young and had wonderfully youthful physical features, including attractive skin and hair, she enjoyed sex less because she was "fat." Her surgery and her hard work following surgery to maintain (and further reduce) her weight was, for Karen, a life choice that had a number of positive consequences. She became, in her mind, a more attractive-looking woman in midlife with respect to her weight. Now, she could look at herself and affirm her appearance, and this then worked to help her feel good about herself and enjoy some of the activities she had previously avoided, including a sexual relationship with her husband.

In Karen's case, sexuality improved as she got older because of life choices that she made that gave her permission to feel good about her sexuality. There are many other aspects about being older that can be fun and fulfilling if one is able to let go of the need to return to or recapture the lifestyle of youth. For example, there are social experiences that one can take advantage of, such as senior discounts, senior activities, travel groups of the American Association of Retired Persons (AARP), and other senior-specific organizations such as senior citizen centers.

The stereotypical notion of a senior citizen center as a warehouse for the discarded older person should be challenged by incorporating some senior activities into your life. In fact, senior citizen centers have become a dominant social and emotional resource for older adults who want to remain engaged through organized programs and activities that involve others in their local neighborhoods and community. State and national support for senior citizen centers is growing exponentially. On a national level, senior citizen centers are one of the mainstays of political activism, particularly on issues related to the needs of older citizens. Senior citizen centers are a source of senior activities including a wide range of special interests. Although bingo, bridge, and free lunches have historically defined senior citizen centers, their reach and breadth of support for those who are older who wish to remain engaged with others in the local community has substantially expanded. Making a life choice that helps you to become involved in senior-specific activities, like senior citizen centers, can be a resource for connections, skill development, personal satisfaction, and well-being in old age that are central components of Positive Aging.

Cultivating Flexibility

Age-related change impacts more than your appearance. It affects your stamina and your strength as well. Even for the most resilient individuals, the effects of aging on functional performance are noticeable. This can be seen in almost every physical sport.

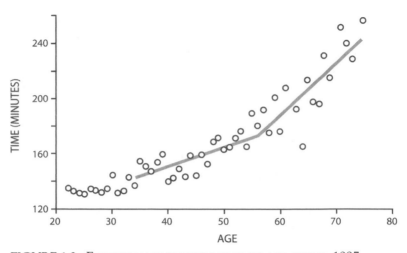

FIGURE 1.2. FASTEST MALE RUNNERS IN EACH AGE GROUP, 1997 BOSTON MARATHON. ADAPTED FROM WILLIAMS, R. K. (1998). "'USE IT OR LOSE IT:' CAN WE SLOW THE EFFECTS OF PHYSICAL DECLINE AS WE AGE." *MARATHON BEYOND* 2, MARCH/APRIL, 34–38.

Figure 1.2 records the average running times for males competing in the Boston Marathon.

In this graph, age-related change shows up in the predictable way. Young runners ages 20 to 30 are fast and they improve through training and practice. Most professional runners know that they will become slower with advancing age, so sustaining a competitive running time must take into consideration the influence of aging on performance, to preserve the ability and motivation to continue to compete and to win.

To think that you could run the Boston Marathon in 200 minutes and maintain that time year after year until you are 65 is not a flexible or realistic strategy. In fact, not dissimilar to other strength and endurance sports, marathon runners who are the best at the sport are expert in applying a flexible approach to training and competition. The sport of marathon running has even assumed a more flexible approach for defining who can win at this sport. For example, if you peruse the newspaper to find out who won the last Boston Marathon, you will note that there are age ranges (or groupings) within which running times are reported. Runners in a given age grouping compete against one another; a 27-year-old runner does not compete against someone who is 80 years old, even though they both have competed in the Boston Marathon on the same day. Competition among age groupings is considered not only unrealistic, but unfair and silly. An 80-year-old runner would not be disappointed if she or he crossed the finish line after a 27-year-old runner. The 80-year-old is paying attention to others in his or her age group as the prime competitor. This relativistic approach to marathon running, which is ubiquitous across almost every competitive sport, allows winning times to be officially counted in age groupings. Using a flexibility strategy such as this, then, is how personal winning remains possible across a marathoner's life span.

Your personal effort to develop the Positive Aging strategy of flexibility involves thinking and feeling in ways that move you away from maladaptive pattern of thinking. Positive Agers challenge negative stylistics embedded in the failure to be flexible, including pessimism, regret, rigidity, self-absorption, worry, and negativity. Positive Agers know how to think and feel flexibly by nurturing life-span skills such as gratitude, forgiveness, and altruism—to be described later—that transcend age and allow you to find happiness irrespective of where you are chronologically along the life-span continuum. Those who practice flexibility are among the happiest in old age.

Focusing on the Positives

Emphasizing the positives versus the negatives of growing old is an important component of Positive Aging. But, like the other Positive Aging characteristics, the ability to focus on the positives does not come without some practice and effort. The nature of this skill involves disentangling what is good about growing old from the bad, and then accentuating it in a situation with another person, or even with oneself. This can occur at two levels.

The first level in emphasizing the positive is simply identifying what is good about old age and then paying attention to it. For example, when you are old and female you probably don't have the responsibility of bearing or rearing a child. For some, passing this phase of life can be quite unsettling, and science has made it possible for women who are older and older to conceive children. These women, however, are the exception and not the rule. In a

New York Times article (Gross, 2007) when middle-aged women were asked what it was they found positive in later life, a number endorsed the idea of being past the childbearing age.

The second way that you can focus on the positives in old age is through the process of reconstrual or reframing. People often reconstrue events, circumstances, and situations. In politics, this is called "spinning." It is a common psychological technique for turning the meaning of events around. There is an adage that a positive person can make lemonade out of lemons. This saying asserts that the person who can do this knows that maintaining a focus on the positive is important to sustaining well-being. When one is old, it is more likely that one will be confronted with an illness that causes physical discomfort or an unanticipated loss of a loved one. The realities of old age are sometimes harsh and the fact that we all are marching through the "four Ds" ensures that there will be some suffering along the way. The important point here is that it is possible to learn and then to actively apply strategies that reconstruct events as a way to optimize how you view being old by moving the meaning of events from a negative to a positive valence. In other words, Positive Aging is construing growing old as meaningful and worthwhile regardless of the challenges that old age inevitably presents. George Valliant (2005) underscored the importance of the skill of reconstrual. He recorded the words of one of his study participants, a 55-year-old poet who attempted to capture the process of finding well-being even in dying:

> A 55-year-old Study poet underscored the dignity even in dying. He rhetorically asked, "What's the difference between a guy who at his final conscious moments before death has a nostalgic grin on his face, as if to say, 'Boy, I sure squeezed that lemon' and another man who fights for every last breath in an effort to turn back to some nagging unfinished business?" Damned if I know, but I sure think it's worth thinking about. (p. 15)

By practicing reframing, you can find peace of mind and well-being even in some of the most challenging circumstances. Those who develop this skill are able to find satisfaction in the presence of age-related decline.

III. A POSITIVE AGING APPLICATION OF THE RECOVERY OF MEANING

How can you find meaning in old age when a personal tragedy enters the picture to cloud your sense of the future? A stroke can do this. Stroke is a cardiovascular insult wherein a blood vessel that carries oxygen and nutrients to the brain either is blocked by a clot or bursts. As this occurs the part of the brain that receives nutrients through this vessel cannot get the blood and oxygen it needs, so it dies. Why a stroke occurs and how it impacts function is complex; however, there are risk factors that predispose a person to stroke. One of these is aging, with the risk for stroke essentially doubling every decade after age 55. At least 66% of all people who have a stroke are 65 years or older.

The following case history is that of an older woman who experienced a stroke as an unintended consequence of aging and was able to regain her meaning by mobilizing resources through the application of the principles of SOC. This example highlights the synergy for coping and finding meaning that comes from the characteristics of Positive Aging.

CAROL'S RECOVERY FROM A STROKE

Carol was a 68-year-old married woman who had lived most of her life free from disease. After she retired at 65, Carol became very active in her neighborhood. In the eyes of many she was a source of emotional and physical support and Carol derived great meaning from this. She had an uncanny way of knowing when people were in need of help and was almost always the first to step in with aid. On a sunny Friday afternoon, as Carol was driving to a local community event, she became dizzy. When she arrived home she telephoned her husband, who left work and rushed Carol to the hospital. Carol had developed a blood clot in her leg that passed through her heart and into her brain, precipitating a stroke. She survived, but it left her entirely paralyzed on her left side, with no feeling in her arm and paralysis in her face. After months of rehabilitation some of her functioning returned, but the stroke had caused permanent facial paralysis and nerve damage in her left arm and leg. Carol was left, for the first time in her life, to contemplate growing old in the presence of substantial impairment.

Carol was always fond of her appearance and felt like she looked 10 years younger than her actual age. Her stroke changed all of that. Her facial paralysis distorted her appearance, which made her fearful to encounter people, even those she knew well. She did not want to leave her house for fear that she might encounter someone who would look at her and cringe. Her role as the neighborhood helper ceased, even though she had fond memories of herself as a helper. She was now the one in need of help. For a period of time Carol became essentially helpless, was reluctant to make contact with her neighbors, and shunned her children's efforts to help her.

One neighbor in particular was determined not to let Carol waste away. This neighbor developed a naturalistic strategy for Carol to re-connect with others through the use of SOC. The neighbor knew that, in the past, Carol had enjoyed preparing baked goods for others, so the neighbor suggested that Carol might consider trying to recover this skill. At first, Carol thought that this was ridiculous. "Can't you see what shape I'm in! You want me to bake cookies?" The neighbor ac-knowledged that Carol would not be able to bake cookies like she used to, but with some restructuring Carol could still do it. Carol was mod-estly interested, but still viewed the whole idea as overwhelming. With Carol's permission, the neighbor met with Carol's daughter and to-gether they came up with a list whereby they broke down the task of baking cookies into three categories: (a) things Carol could do by her-self, (b) things that she could do with help, (c) things that she simply could not do. They showed the list to Carol, who immediately fixated on the first category with the thought, "Well, yes, I can still hold a measuring cup in my right hand." This was what the neighbor had hoped, since some of the tasks were simple and she had watched Carol do these in the recent past. The daughter became important, since she was the person who assisted Carol to perform the tasks listed in the second category. The neighbor unobtrusively performed those tasks that Carol could not do (e.g., removing cookies from the hot oven). After several tries, Carol was able to bake several batches of cookies. The first were poorly made, but they got better as Carol got more comfortable with the task. For the first time, Carol began to realize that she could still do some of the things that had given her meaning in the past.

Once the cookies were baked, the neighbor then suggested taking them to Carol's other neighbors as gifts. With some coaxing, Carol decided that this sounded doable, particularly as the neighbor once again broke the task down for Carol into three categories: (a) can do, (b) can do with help, and (c) can't do. The neighbor also added additional structure to the first category: (a) things Carol can already do well and (b) things Carol can do better with practice. Not all of the tasks involved physical coordination. Carol was still afraid to approach her neighbors for fear that some "would cringe and not want these awful cookies," but her daughter challenged Carol's assumption and suggested that this was something that she "could physically do" although it might be emotionally difficult. Carol soon began to realize that she was facing some of her fears. So the daughter agreed to help Carol deliver the cookies and to provide a safety net should neighbors react badly. As Carol engaged in this routine, she began a pattern of baking cookies and delivering them to neighbors. The task lists began to shift in favor of Carol's independent behavior as Carol became stronger and more able. No neighbors reacted badly; in fact several caught on to the strategy and began to expect Carol to bake them cookies. This helped Carol rediscover her meaning as a helper.

Carol's story is a good example of how SOC can be applied to help you rediscover your meaning in old age in disablement. Yes, for Carol, things will never be the same. She may never be able to walk again unaided, her face will likely not recover from its paralysis, and the damage to her brain and cardiovascular system may make her more susceptible to another stroke or premature death. These issues initially caused a sense of hopelessness in Carol. Her neighbor and daughter, however, helped her derive meaning from her situation through the process of reconstrual using SOC. Even though Carol felt helpless, there were things that she could still do. She could move and she could still communicate, and she was able to engage in some simple behaviors that could be used to reengage her in cooking. Using SOC, one task—baking cookies—was *selected* for Carol to relearn. Baking cookies was then broken down into three separate components that increased incrementally in level of difficulty. Carol practiced each of these until she became proficient in their performance (*optimization*). Carol *compensated* for deficits on those behaviors that she could no longer do with only a single hand by relying on the assistance of her neighbor and her daughter, and by using specialized utensils designed for single-hand manipulation.

Carol and her daughter worked together to identify additional chores that Carol could engage in (*selectivity*). Although Carol could not negotiate the stairs to the basement where her laundry was sorted, she could fold a basket of laundry with one hand if it was upstairs (*compensation*). Eventually, Carol improved her ability to perform household chores and address her routine needs, including learning to drive short distances to run errands (*optimization*), and in doing so regained her sense of competency, and began to feel that her life had meaning.

Carol's stroke and her recovery efforts had unanticipated benefits. For one, she developed a more meaningful relationship with her daughter. Although they lived near each other, Carol's daughter had been engaged in her own life and its challenges. The stroke was a tragedy, and at first Carol wanted to be separated from everyone. Once she decided to reengage herself, however, Carol's daughter had the opportunity to help her. When Carol allowed her daughter to do this, it allowed them to build a closer relationship.

Chapter 2

STRATEGY #2: YOU'RE NEVER
TOO OLD TO LEARN

I. LEARNING IN LATER LIFE

Learning is an important Positive Aging strategy to help you remain vital in your later years. To follow the adage of Henry Ford: "Anyone who stops learning is old, whether at twenty or eighty. Anyone who keeps learning stays young. The greatest thing in life is to keep your mind young."

In youth, formal schooling provides younger people with knowledge and skills that make them marketable in society and improve their social standing. For older people, learning has been prescribed as a way to preserve intellectual functioning and stave off age-related memory decline. By way of analogy, a popular phrase associated with physical exercise is "Use it or lose it"; that is, not only should you exercise to keep your body in shape, but if you don't exercise you could lose whatever fitness you have acquired. "Use it or lose it" now also applies to brain health and research indicates that working your brain not only makes you smarter but may also preserve your mental faculties (Ball, Berch, Helmers, Jobe, & Leveck, 2002).

How does learning preserve your mental abilities, and *why*? There is strong evidence that staying intellectually engaged helps sustain a wide array of cognitive processes including attention and memory

(Hultsch, Hertzog, Small, & Dixon, 1999). Using SOC as described in Chapter 1, learning can compensate for age deficits (Park, Gutchess, Mead, & Stine-Morrow, 2007). There is another reason to pursue learning in old age: the process of continuing education helps you remain in contact with others and stay up-to-date in your ever-changing world. Learning is a tested strategy for avoiding personal isolation as a result of intellectual obsolescence. Erik Erikson, a pioneering theorist in adult life-span development, understood this concept in the 1980s when he asserted that older people should remain in the system of formal education to stay vital in later life. Conversely, he believed that older people would help formal education stay vital (Erikson, Erikson, & Kivnick, 1986).

> It is impossible to stress too strongly how important it is that the educational system . . . make lifelong learning available to everyone. . . . Ideally, all higher education courses should be open to elders who bring enthusiasm and interesting perspectives into the classroom. (p. 315)

Like Erikson, life-span scholars have advocated for the continued pursuit of learning into old and even very old age because this intellectual and social renewal allows us to refine our interests and curiosities, as well as to sustain our drive for discovery and mastery. Lifelong learning is needed in the 21st century when so much new information is being disseminated every day.

Avenues for new learning and exploration are endless. If you want to learn about our universe, the Internet can open a whole new means to do this. In just minutes, a learner can find him or herself surveying the surface of Mars through the Mars orbiter and lander that have been streaming pictures and information about Mars to us on Earth for years. The Hubble telescope has cataloged innumerable observations of the universe including distant stars and nebulae. All of this information is easily available through the Internet, as it is to scientists and astronomers who are engaged in the pioneering work of surveying our solar system and mapping the universe.

Our homes are now vast libraries that can receive knowledge in many formats and contexts, including radio, television, print media, the Internet, and interactive computer-based technologies, such as web cams and digital television, which allows the viewer to respond to learning exercises through touch-screen technology and real-time communications. Devices now exist that can simulate virtual classrooms in one's own home and can connect villages in the remotest corner of the world to your television or computer. This knowledge transformation holds great promise for adults who want to be learners in later life and stay abreast of the issues in the world.

Despite all of these learning innovations, stereotypes of old-age obsolescence persist. Among them are:

- You can't teach an old dog new tricks.
- Older people can't learn without help.
- When you are old it's hard to accept new ideas and ways of thinking.
- The aging brain has no capacity for new learning.
- Alzheimer's disease destroys your ability to learn.

Like all stereotypes, these statements contain a grain of truth, partly because—unlike those in younger generations—older people grew up in an educational system where learning was guided by specific traditions and age-biased assumptions, such as:

- Learning occurs at a specific place and time.
- To learn you must possess the attributes of youth.
- You learn what you are told to learn.

The first age-biased assumption comes from the traditional use of the formal structures of classroom education. The classroom setting is important because it continues to influence our approach to learning. It is a controlled environment that involves an instructor who is a source and facilitator of knowledge. The learner is passive and listens, raises her or his hand when a question arises, works quietly at a desk, and follows the rules of classroom order. Interacting with knowledge is supervised and the most highly rewarded learners in the system are those who conform to this structure. Older learners may have difficulty reverting to such a system. A new approach to learning that challenges this assumption focuses on the comfort of the learner. Optimizing learning means making sure that the learner can concentrate on the subject matter by creating the most comfortable environment possible; this means expanding learning beyond the classroom setting and into the home.

The second age-biased assumption is that to learn you must possess the intellectual attributes of youth. For example, success in the classroom is measured by good grades, and to be a straight A student you must possess a good memory, reading and writing skills, study skills, and test-taking ability. These are learner attributes that blend optimum biology with learning capacity and personal effort. One's memory and attention are best when one is young; one engages in the conscious practice to build academic skills during one's formative years. Assuming you have the right intellect, the more you study, the better you will perform on tests and the more likely you will obtain a high grade. This approach to learning, unfortunately, has constrained many people to believe that learning not only occurs at a specific time and place, but that to be a good learner one must have certain innate characteristics that are related to a sharp intellect and youth.

There is, however, nothing further from the truth. Everyone can learn no matter their resource base or intellectual endowment. Other personal qualities are important for learning including a sense of appreciation, experiences with the world, inquisitiveness, and flexibility in perception and thought. These are qualities that one acquires across the life span and are often enhanced in old age, giving the older learner broader perspective and capability to learn.

The third age-biased learning assumption is that you are told "what" to learn. This is illustrated in the well-known adage that schooling consists of "reading, writing, and arithmetic." These core subject matters that we all have been taught are at the heart of formal education. In such a system a good student performs these tasks well. You can't learn if you can't read, write, or do arithmetic. These topics would seem to favor any person who is motivated to learn. However, in reality, they have biases. For example, an older person with a hearing impairment, a deficit of motor skills, or poor vision may have trouble utilizing these skills even though they can still learn. These proscribed topics also favor compliant learners, that is, those who learn what they are supposed to learn and don't ask questions about why a subject matter is important or relevant.

A related point raised by this assumption is that you must be told "how" to learn. The idea here is that if you can learn how to speak Latin even though it has little practical use, you will have developed the skills to study and master other content areas. It doesn't matter what you learn, only that you develop the skills to learn. These skills can then be applied as you progress through the formal schooling curriculum.

As an older learner, you may question this assumption: Why should I learn to speak Latin or master calculus if I'm not interested in it? Why should I learn all of the names of the presidents of the United States when I have no interest in politics? Being told what or how to learn is not necessarily helpful in later life, especially if you have a sense of what you do and do not want to learn. You probably have enough life experience to discriminate between what is useful and not useful when it comes to the subject matter that interests you.

So, why would you want to continue to learn in later life, when sitting in a classroom in a hard desk chair is not comfortable, when learning requires rapid-response memory and you are somewhat slow to recall details, or when you do not want to be told what to learn and how to learn it?

Contrary to these age-biased assumptions about learning, the data on continuing education suggests that the latter half of the life span may be when the desire to learn is the strongest (Findsen, 2005). However, the approach to learning in later life must take a different form than it had in youth. In response to this fact, whole industries have emerged in recent years that cater to the older learner, among them elder hostel, lifelong living institutes, senior universities, and, more recently, senior Internet networks. These new learning environments make distinctions about learning in later life. One is that although older people are interested in seeking out opportunities for continuing education, their learning needs are different from those of younger people. For example, late-life learners need a medium that matches their learning style and interests. Some older people learn better in contexts where they have more time to study and explore the material and their learning may even improve if time pressure or testing demands are relaxed. Making material meaningful to one's daily living—for example, memorizing a personal identification number—can be important to older people.

Not all learning need be practical. For some, what makes learning rewarding is the chance to follow one's curiosities, and there is no better time to do this than in old age, when the need to use learning to meet social obligations is no longer necessary. Learning as a form of personal fulfillment is more feasible in later life than at any other time in one's life.

To be sure, a new paradigm for learning is needed that matches the proliferating and diverse opportunities that are emerging in late-life learning. This is where Positive Aging comes in.

II. A POSITIVE AGING AND LEARNING

Learning is a Positive Aging strategy that capitalizes on one's motivations to stay intellectually engaged, based on one's personal interests, and drive to renew, discover, and master skills. When you are young, you are curious, you have emerging interests, and your desires for discover and mastery are strong and encouraged. Old people are considered prurient if their curiosity is not held in check. The fact is that children and older people are equally curious. A Positive Aging reframing of this stereotypical dichotomy is that old age is a time in life, like childhood, when you can finally feel free to act on these motivations. For example, in later life you may have more time to think about your world; you have had more experiences with people and things and may have greater reason to ask the "how" and "why" questions about everyday living. The child may be preoccupied by the guiding influence of others, including parents, teachers, and mentors. Young adults may be caught up with achievement pursuits, such as earning money, establishing credibility, and advancing in one's job. A defining feature of a Positive Aging approach to learning is the active pursuit of continuing education as a means of satisfying personal interests and curiosities. This is your opportunity to exercise your true interests and to pursue something simply because you are interested in it or curious about it.

A Positive Aging approach to learning is to examine your beliefs about yourself as a learner. Some of your ideas may be at the basis of your motivation to educate yourself in old age. Ask yourself, prior to pursuing a learning opportunity:

How do I learn?
What do I want to learn?

A critical precursor to the question of "How do I learn?" is your belief that you are still capable of learning, regardless of your age, stage in life, or situation. You may feel that because you are experiencing some deficiencies in your memory that learning is not for you. You may be experiencing some decline in sensory function, including vision or hearing, that causes you to believe that it is more difficult for you to learn. Furthermore, it may be that learning is taxing to your current intellectual stamina and requires too much effort. While there is no denying that some of your faculties become less responsive to challenge or demand as you grow older, and that you may need to invest more effort to learn in some cases than you did when you were younger, this should not preclude your pursuit of learning. In fact, data suggest that simply engaging in a learning experience can have advantages, including protection against age-related cognitive decline and progressive diseases such as Alzheimer's disease.

As a case in point, consider the findings from a study that appeared in the *Journal of the American Medical Association* (Wilson, Barnes, Schneider, et al., 2002), in which over 800 Catholic clergy who were 65 years of age and older were intensively followed for a 5-year period. The goal of this study was to understand more about the kinds of activities that these individuals engaged in that influenced their brain health. Their intellectual functioning was monitored by self-report and observation and they were asked whether they had engaged in any kind of lifestyle practice that involved learning, that is: Were they active in educational and intellectual pursuits?

Participants' responses varied. Some were very intellectually active while others were more or less "brain sedentary." Intellectual engagement was associated with preservation of cognitive functioning and postponement of the emergence of Alzheimer's for those people who were at high risk for the disease.

With regard to the questions of "what" and "where" learning occurred, these Catholic clergy reported a variety of situations including viewing educational television and listening to the radio, reading newspapers and books, playing games such as cards and checkers, and doing crossword puzzles. Some were very involved in mind teaser games (e.g., sudoku). Several participants reported going to museums, movies, and out to dinner on a regular basis. (These were also listed by the researchers as intellectual activities because they construed learning as occurring in all kinds of contexts.)

This expanded list of intellectual activities went far beyond what would stereotypically be found in formal schooling; some activities, like watching TV, might not even be thought of by most people as promoting learning of any kind, even though television watching does require actively applying cognitive skills. In this study, no single activity was particularly beneficial; all contributed to intellectual engagement and preserving cognitive functioning and preventing the onset of Alzheimer's disease. This study illustrated that learning can occur within the context of almost any activity that involves actively thinking about or interacting with your world, and such learning has tangible benefits for maintaining your abilities as you grow old.

Positive Aging characteristics applied to everyday activities and learning can help you remain intellectually active. The characteristics of Positive Aging—namely (a) mobilizing your resources, (b) making affirmative life choices, (c) cultivating flexibility, and (d) focusing on the positives—are the underpinnings of optimal life-span learning. How these work to promote an intellectually engaged lifestyle is described next.

Mobilizing Resources for Learning

Learning, like the other Positive Aging strategies, requires you to expend effort on the task. This means that your desire to learn must be strong enough to motivate you to put effort into the process. There are several steps that affect your motivation to learn: (a) your belief that learning is possible in old age; (b) identifying your curiosities or interests; and (c) knowing your learning strengths and weaknesses.

Beliefs are tightly connected to expectations, and expectations produce behaviors. It is a truism that you are what you think you are. I recall an instructor in one of my graduate classes in social psychology who remarked, "If you want to be famous then begin believing that you are famous. When you do this you will tell everyone you meet that you are famous and it won't be long before you will be famous."

If you believe that you are a learner, you will act like a learner and you will want others to think of you as a learner as well. So, like fame, believing that you can learn will initiate, for you, the learning process. Negative self-statements about learning, even the ones that are based in some truth, can magnify stereotypical age deficits. "I can't learn because my eyesight is poor." This will stop you from pursuing lifelong learning if you think that your learning is dependent on visual acuity that is unimpaired. The fact is that the most persistent barrier to your pursuit of learning is whether you believe that you are a learner or not. If you think you can't learn then you won't act. Others who think that learning occurs mainly in youth might also reinforce this. The following case history demonstrates this:

SALLY AND THE PIANO

Sally, 65 years old, was a career civil service employee for most of her adult life. She started working for the federal government when she was young. At the time, because a college degree was not needed to get her job, she chose to drop out of college to pursue full-time work. Her husband followed a similar path and had been a mail carrier for the U.S. Postal Service for 30 years before he retired. Both Sally and her husband had no history of higher education such as degrees, credentials, or licenses, although their long and dedicated work history had resulted in a healthy retirement income. Most of their hobbies involved outdoor activities with their children: boating, camping, and hiking. When Sally's mother passed away Sally inherited a small upright piano from her mother's estate. Sally remembered this piano from when she was growing up and recalled a great interest in learning how to play it. Because her mother and father had few resources, they could not afford lessons for Sally, so she never pursued her interests. Now that the piano belonged to Sally, she was surprised that she still had an interest in learning how to play. At age 65, however, she reasoned that it was too late to act on her interests, even though her motivation was strong. She spoke to her husband about it and he encouraged her to consider learning to play the piano. He said, "Sally, you only live once and if you want to do something, I say go for it." She then called her brother to get his opinion. His view was quite different from her husband's. Her brother had wanted this piano when their mother died because he had several granddaughters who desired to learn to play the piano, so the brother had some bitterness that Sally was given the piano. Her brother said, "Sally, this is a dumb idea. Think of all the money it would cost. Aren't you too old to be learning a musical instrument anyway? Even if you do try to learn it, you will be dead long before you get good at playing and your arthritis will make it difficult for you to keep up the pace of practicing. I suggest you spend your money on one of your grandchildren who could really benefit from learning to play." Sally agreed with her brother and let the matter drop. She asked her grandchildren if any of them would be interested in learning to play the piano but no one took her up on her offer.

What could Sally do to cultivate a better mind-set for acting on her desire to learn to play the piano? First, she could examine her beliefs about her ability to learn and, specifically, identify those that prevented her from pursuing her interest. In Sally's case, she believed her brother's criticism that she was throwing her money away on the foolish pursuit of learning to play a musical instrument when she did not have enough years of life left to become proficient. The expectation to become proficient concerned Sally. Her brother defined "success" as only playing well, and Sally internalized her brother's idea. Whether realistic or not, this inflated expectation created a barrier for Sally. A Positive Aging approach to learning to play the piano might involve Sally using a more selective and flexible definition of success. She might enjoy the challenge and the incremental steps toward acquiring the ability to play the piano, however small. The fact that Sally, through learning, could start to recognize the meaning of musical notes and connecting these to a larger musical score might be inherently rewarding. Like most people, proficiency comes with practice and effort, along with the expectation that one can master some aspects of a task. What might be more productive is for Sally to mobilize her resources to improve her abilities as a result of the learning process. This would be a more modest way to approach a learning task that Sally was curious about.

If she was interested in measuring actual improvement in her playing, an innovative strategy might be for Sally to tape-record her efforts and then replay the tape at different points in time as she progressed through her lessons. What follows is a realistic list of expectations:

- Being able to read the notes on a musical cleft
- Learning to match the notes on paper to specific piano keys

- The ability to play a series of notes from a musical score
- Being able to play a series of notes at the proper tempo

It is quite possible that, through tracking her progress, Sally would generate evidence that her piano playing was improving and that her age was not a barrier to learning.

Learning as an Affirmative Life Choice

Learning, like physical exercise, is most effective when you develop a habit or a pattern of doing it. If you haven't been involved in learning and you decide to start, it may require some initial effort. Over time, and if you persist, it will become easier to do and you will gain satisfaction from the outcome. If Sally were to engage in learning to play the piano, she would begin to acquire a new skill. This would require persistence and sustained effort on her part. She would discover aspects of piano playing that came easily to her and she would also confront challenges that would require her to expend additional effort to work through. Along the way, as she persisted in playing through regular practice, she would likely improve at piano playing and as she did, the value that she placed on this learning activity would increase. Although the benefits from learning will come with time, learning almost always involves persistence and patience. If you are trying to acquire a new skill like piano playing, you will make many mistakes and you will need to recover from setbacks. There are setbacks that may, in part, be due to the aging process. For example, if you are trying to learn to play a new piece that requires speeded performance, you may encounter some difficulty due to deficits in fine-motor dexterity. There is scientific evidence that short-term memory deteriorates with age. Therefore, you may find that you are not as quick to learn a score or link notes to piano keys as someone who is half your age. Sight-reading music might progress a little slower, and you may have to restrict the number of pieces that you learn. To keep your motivation up to continue to practice the piano, you must make this decision a life choice. This may involve finding ways to use your emerging piano-playing ability. Volunteering to play at your local senior center or in contexts where it is needed, such as in a school classroom or at a nursing home, may help you to sustain your efforts.

Cultivating Flexibility for Learning

In Sally's case she correctly links the "how to" in learning to practice and recognizing progress. Often, when a person studies a new topic, the recognition of improvement involves establishing a timeline and noting benchmarks. Sally can experience the joy associated with making gains in learning to play the piano without necessarily becoming proficient. This kind of flexibility, which is the third characteristic of Positive Aging, is an important step in a Positive Aging approach to learning.

Positive Agers use flexibility to challenge ageist stereotypes, such as those highlighted in Sally's story, by finding ways to give themselves permission to engage in a task in which they are interested. So, instead of assuming, "I'm too old to learn," a Positive Ager might reframe this as, "Because I'm old, I can use new learning to preserve my capabilities and keep myself mentally fit." Instead of concluding, "I already know what I need to know," a Positive Ager might say, "Although I know many things, there are always new things to learn."

In the exercise below, examine your own beliefs about learning with the goal of identifying those that keep you from engaging in an activity which interests you.

- Identify a learning activity that you would like to start, but haven't.
- Write down two assumptions that prevent you from engaging in it.
- Generate some affirmative statements that challenge these assumptions.
- Come up with an alternative rationale to give yourself permission to engage in this activity.

Age-Friendly Settings for Learning

There are emerging settings specifically designed for older learners. Three age-friendly learning contexts are described below: Elderhostel, lifelong learning institutes, and senior Internet networks.

1. Elderhostel

Elderhostel is one of the largest not-for-profit educational organizations in the United States for adults who are 50 years of age and older.

It was founded in 1975 by David Bianco and Martin Knowlton, two professors at the University of New Hampshire (UNH). They set out to create an instructional context that focused on learning for the fun of it. Since they both enjoyed traveling and felt that this was an excellent way to learn, they began sponsoring courses, lectures, and workshops that focused not only on travel, but on opportunities that travel afforded for learning new things. For example, to learn about art, why not do so by traveling to Paris, France, and touring the Louvre? To learn about the history of the Civil War, why not tour many of the settings in the South where the Civil War occurred, including visiting museums and libraries where Civil War memorabilia and records are kept. Below are examples of a range of Elderhostel programs that include both domestic and international travel.

THE WORLD IS OUR CLASSROOM

National Programs

- Attend the Ashland, Oregon Independent Film Festival to meet filmmakers and directors of independently made documentaries, features, and shorter works.
- Travel on a Mississippi River paddleboat to a variety of cities including Memphis, Tennessee and New Orleans, Louisiana to learn about the history of the South.
- Follow the trail of Lewis and Clark, and discover their contribution to American history.
- Travel through Colorado by way of historic trains and study the evolution of the railroad industry and its role in the settling of Colorado.
- Learn about American independence through a series of field trips, including a walking tour of the historic center of Boston, Massachusetts.

International Programs

- Visit the villages where the artist Claude Monet lived, and learn about his life and work at various historical sites and museums in France.

- Study the history and culture of India by visiting ancient forts, temples, and palaces in several major cities, such as New Delhi.
- Attend lectures by local scholars from Poland and the Czech Republic to learn more about social transitions in these nations.
- Hike the Fundy Trail and travel the back roads of Quebec's townships to learn about the history and social structure of Quebec.
- Visit Kenya to learn about local effects of global warming, such as the shrinking water supply and the changing climate. Interact with local indigenous peoples to learn about the African view of the Western world.

Since its inception, Elderhostel has been very popular enrolling nearly 200,000 people yearly. It has locations in all 50 United States, where it offers more than 8,000 programs. The goal of Elderhostel is to make learning fun and meaningful for any person, regardless of age or situation. It gives older people a chance to find new friends while at the same time satisfying their curiosity and interests. It is likely that Elderhostel will grow substantially as the health and well-being of older people improve and active life span is lengthened (http://www.elderhostel.org/).

2. Lifelong Learning Institutes

A context designed specifically for older learners was conceived over two decades ago by Bernard Osher, a wealthy businessman and philanthropist who was very committed to lifelong education. He identified a need for an educational curriculum that specifically addressed older adults. Through his foundation, Osher established grants and strategic initiatives with universities and colleges for creating an extended learning environment that was tailored to older adults. One of the first Osher lifelong learning institutes (OLLI) was established in Maine through coordinating resources using the Maine Senior College Network, an organization that involves 15 colleges committed to providing peer-taught courses, workshops, and other activities to learners ages 55 years and older. The mission of the OLLI in Maine is to "provide a curriculum of intellectually stimulating learning opportunities and special activities." Many of the teachers are emeritus university professors and retired teacher volunteers from the community college and public education sector. However, you don't need a degree to be a OLLI instructor. You just need to possess some unique knowledge or skills that would be of interest to others.

The OLLI concept has been widely adopted by higher education nationally and there are institutes associated with universities and state colleges in California, Florida, Maryland, and Utah, to name just a few. The OLLI in California, managed through the University of California at San Francisco (UCSF), provides training and programs that focus on health and the health sciences as these relate to aging. Targeted courses that are part of the UCSF OLLI include health care issues that involve wellness education for senior adults as well as courses that focus on health problems in the elderly (e.g., osteoporosis). This highlights one of the unique features of the OLLI in isolating those issues that are of special interest to the senior community.

3. SeniorNet

SeniorNet is a tailored online service that is specifically for seniors. It grew out of a research project funded by the Markle Foundation in 1986 to determine if computers and telecommunications could enhance the lives of older adults. Since then it has built a worldwide infrastructure that is composed of computer users who are 50 years and older who enjoy exploring Internet technology and interacting with others about it. For a modest yearly membership fee, SeniorNet provides a variety of online computer services as well as courses and live instructor-led workshops. This occurs in over 200 learning centers throughout the United States. SeniorNet has helped literally millions of older adults use the computer and Internet. It publishes a regular e-newsletter and has an extensive online learning curriculum that is part of its learning centers. It also offers, among other things, discounts on computer-related equipment and even holds regional conferences where people can meet face-to-face and share ideas. SeniorNet also operates an educational Web site that shares information and technical support for computer and programming issues. It also acts as a warehouse for learning across a wide range of technical topics. Following is a description of SeniorNet from its Web page:

SENIORNET MISSION STATEMENT
(ADAPTED FROM WEB PAGE)
Provides older adults with education and access to computer technologies to enhance their lives.

SeniorNet is an independent, international, volunteer-based nonprofit organization that is one of the world's leading technology educators of adults 50+. SeniorNet has an international membership of computer users, hosts a thriving online community, and hosts a network of locally operated Learning Centers throughout the United States and internationally.

These are just three of a growing number of new and innovative settings for learning that are age friendly. As you explore these new venues, some may work better for you than others. Testing how you learn in different contexts and through various mediums is also part of the learning process itself. As you evaluate what contexts work best for you, you will not only develop flexibility, but you will be engaging in a process of affirming learning as something that you can do in later life.

Focusing on the Positives

In later life learning is optional. Therefore, learning can be a hobby or a leisure pursuit; it is not work even though you may work very hard to learn something. The metaphor of how a person expends energy in both work and play is useful here. In work, the process may not be intrinsically rewarding, but the outcome of gainful employment yields money, health insurance, and other benefits. Money is rewarding because it can be traded for wants and needs. Many people endure work to acquire money. At the same time, play involves an expenditure of effort but is more intrinsically rewarding. We choose who, where, and how we expend our energy and our money when we play.

This juxtaposition between work and play is a centerpiece in the well-known story of Tom Sawyer by Mark Twain:

> Saturday morning was come, and all the summer world was bright and fresh. . . . Tom appeared on the sidewalk with a bucket of whitewash and a long-handled brush . . . a deep melancholy settled down upon his spirit. Thirty yards of board fence. . . . Life to him seemed hollow, and existence but a burden. . . . Ben Rogers hove in sight presently. . . . Tom contemplated the boy. . . . [Tom said to Ben] "What do you call work?"

[Ben said to Tom] "Why, aint that work?" Tom resumed whitewashing and answered . . . "All I know is it suits Tom Sawyer." [Ben says to Tom] "[Do you] Like it?" "Well I don't see why I ought'nt to like it." "Does a boy get a chance to whitewash a fence every day?" This put the thing in a new light. . . . Presently [Ben said,] "Say, Tom, let me whitewash a little." "Ben, I'd like to, honest injun; . . . well, Jim wanted to do it, but she [Aunt Polly] wouldn't let him; Sid wanted to do it and she wouldn't let Sid." [Ben said,] "Oh, shuck, I'll be as careful. Now lemme try." . . . Tom gave up the brush with reluctance in his face but alacrity in his heart. (pp. 13–15)

In the story, Tom Sawyer is charged to work and he clearly views it with gloom and drudgery. To solve this dilemma, he comes up with a strategy to make his "work" seem like "fun" and valuable to others. He assumes an affirmative mind-set and translates this to his friend, Ben. Once this mind-set is in place, whitewashing becomes appealing to Ben. This story teaches the lesson that how we construe a task influences our motivation to engage in it. If the task is learning and we view learning as valuable, we will be motivated to engage in it.

Below are a few Positive Aging reasons that older adults pursue educational experiences:

- Learning is how I become more engaged with others.
- I like learning because it opens up new ways of thinking and relating to the world.
- It's fun to learn new things.
- I enjoy the challenge of acquiring a new skill.
- Learning makes me feel more youthful.
- When I learn, I challenge the saying "You can't teach an old dog new tricks."

III. LEARNING IN LONG-TERM CARE

This chapter has focused on learning in old age based on the assumption that the older learner is relatively healthy and is cognitively intact. But what about lifelong learning among people with memory impairment? Does learning cease when a person becomes cognitively impaired? Most people would assume that it does. This conclusion, however intuitively appealing, restricts the possibility that learning in some shape or form is still possible at any age and in any condition. In reality, learning in such a context just depends on how you construe what learning is. For this reason it may be useful to extend a Positive Aging approach to learning into a context that you would ordinarily not think it belongs.

The assumption that learning is no longer possible when a person becomes cognitively impaired is one of the most persistent forms of ageism that exists in our society. This stereotype has prevented many older people from experiencing the benefits of Positive Aging through learning in advanced age. Our society accepts the fact that learning occurs in younger people who are intellectually challenged. Among this group of younger people, many of whom qualify for special education services, the impetus for learning is particularly strong. So, why can't learning still occur for people who have dementia?

A careful examination of what goes on in long-term care facilities, including geriatric residential care centers, assisted living facilities, board-and-care facilities, and nursing homes is that cognitively impaired people are simply cared for. Learning, exploration, the satisfying of curiosities, and the drive to discover may still continue, but it is difficult to engineer experiences for learning in these contexts. The contention of Positive Aging is that learning in these situations can still occur, although how learning manifests itself may be somewhat different for people in these settings. As a context that is a learning environment in both older and younger groups, consider art. It would be surprising to find an accredited long-term care facility that did not have a program for art involving body movement, music appreciation, and drawing. For youth these activities would be construed as learning, but for memory impaired older adults they are often viewed as time fillers. Is the older woman who is cognitively impaired and struggling to draw a picture on a piece of paper learning or is she simply going through some overly rehearsed behavior that is meaningless to her or to others around her? This is an interesting question that requires thinking about learning at a deeper level, as is highlighted in the following example.

DE KOONING AND ALZHEIMER'S DISEASE

Willem de Kooning (April 24, 1904–March 19, 1997) was born in Rotterdam in the Netherlands. He is famous for his abstract impressionist works, particularly his portrayal of the female form. In the 1980's, de Kooning was diagnosed with Alzheimer's disease (AD) and as the disease progressed, the style of his paintings began to change. There was substantial debate over whether his later paintings, which became clean, sparse, and graphic, were works of art or merely meaningless manifestations of his deteriorating mental condition. Regardless, from 1980 to 1990, de Kooning continued to paint prolifically. For some experts this era of his painting was viewed as supremely successful. Others judged his work as worthless, including the Museum of Modern Art, who deemed that his mental state severely affected his ability to paint coherently and would not show these works (Fact Monster, 2007).

Was de Kooning continuing to create and follow his curiosities and interests in the presence of Alzheimer's Disease (AD) or was his mind simply gone, with his hand drawing randomly on the canvas?

This anecdote about de Kooning highlights the dilemma associated with learning and creating when one is cognitively impaired. It is of course naive to assume AD will not impact learning; however, a Positive Aging view would place value on de Kooning's continued participation in his art and the influence his disease had on his artistic expression as he continued to derive meaning from it.

Therapeutically learning is useful in the presence of disease-related cognitive impairment because it opens the possibility to invent techniques and strategies that capitalize on the self-enhancement process. An innovative approach based on the idea that learning is sustained in AD is becoming a part of the curriculum of some long-term care facilities. They are applying Montessori methods to facilitate learning in older adults with AD.

Cameron Camp (2006), a research psychologist, has found success in improving the quality of life for people with AD using Montessori, an approach to learning in preschool and elementary school children that encourages doing graded tasks that use motor skills involving the five sensory processes. Camp was motivated by the possibility that cognitively impaired people still have intellectual capacities such as curiosity, creativity, and other forms of exploration and that many sensory processes, such as touch and smell, are still intact in diseases of aging. He proposed that although the range of these capacities is restricted, by using the Montessori method of failure-free learning by doing, life satisfaction and well-being could be optimized. In study after study, Camp demonstrated increases in positive affect and decreases in problematic behaviors in older people with AD who participated in Montessori learning. The Montessori method for older, cognitively impaired adults is based on the following five principles:

- Learning is optimized in a cooperative environment that incorporates positive peer interaction.
- The goal of learning is to foster responsible and adaptive people who are lifelong learners.
- Learning takes place through multiple sensory mediums that are activated through the physical manipulation of materials.
- Learning requires the integration of social, emotional, aesthetic, spiritual, and cognitive domains. The whole person is considered.
- Respect and caring are at the foundation of the educational curriculum.

This exercise creates an opportunity for the person to explore familiar materials in meaningful ways and interact with others as a consequence of the process. These activities have the potential to preserve recognition memory as well as build a sense of achievement and accomplishment in older persons. The underlying goal is to provide opportunities to help people engage in their world in an interactive and involved way, and in so doing retain unique abilities that distinguished them as meaningful individuals in earlier stages of the life span.

Chapter 3

STRATEGY #3: YOU CAN USE THE PAST TO CULTIVATE WISDOM

I. VALUING THE PAST

Life moves forward, and as it does we age. As we age we change. This can occur internally through the natural evolution of our psychological selves. Change can also come from the outside when events in our day-to-day living shape our life routines. Sources of change can come from within or without, can be positive or negative, but either way, they work to make us different as we grow older.

Paradoxically, we also create stability as we age. Life-span stability is based on rehearsed patterns of thinking, feeling, and behaving. It is from these predictable cycles that we derive meaning. Humans take comfort in knowing the consequences of their behavior. The process of growing older especially in our later years reinforces who we are and our comfort level with our everyday circumstances. Long-term stability in our self-perceptions, and how we feel toward others and our living situation, engenders a special sense of unity that connects our past to our present and brings us peace of mind. This stability-change dialectic also influences how we anticipate our future, including our hopes, dreams, and desires. It is this connectedness with the three dimensions of time—the past, the present, and the future—that must be understood if we want to be happy in old age and experience Positive Aging.

I was reminded of this fact during a recent visit to the Yonghe (or Llama) Temple in Beijing, China. Not unlike other tourists who travel to Beijing, I had placed the Llama Temple high on my list of sights to see. Entering the temple grounds I was struck by the magnificence of the structure, not in terms of its size or beauty, but in its organization and the wisdom of its architecture. Of the five main buildings composing the temple, the Hall of Harmony and Peace was of most interest to me. In this hall there stood three large Buddhas who, according to their inscription, represented the three positions of time. The Gautama or center Buddha was the "present." To the right was the Kasyapa Matanga Buddha (the past). To the left was the Maitreya Buddha (the future). Facing each Buddha were small meditation altars with a pillow at the base for kneeling. I noted the ongoing worshipping of the Chinese who were intermingled with tourists. Around the Buddhas the behavior of worship was manifest in the wear of the pillows, which pointed to the popularity of each Buddha. The pillow for the Maitreya Buddha (the future) was frayed and heavily worn in the center. During my visit I observed several groups of people simultaneously kneeling on the Maitreya Buddha (future) pillow burning incense, chanting, and praying. Activity was less intense for the pillow in front of the Gautama Buddha (present), which was also worn, but in better condition. The Kasyapa Mtanga (past) pillow seemed nearly new and there was no sign of activity around it; no incense burning, no flowers, no prayers. Few seemed interested in Kasyapa Matanga. The wear evident in the pillows of the Buddhas symbolizing the present and the future suggested that worshippers were concentrating on different issues in life's journey. Divine help was being sought for circumstances occupying worshippers' current situations and their future; perhaps these were matters of health, family problems, or other dilemmas. I wondered if this focus may have been at the expense of missing some wisdom from the past. Can what we have experienced and encountered in the past help us navigate the future? Or is the past an inert body of information that should be disregarded as we move on with the business of living?

These questions are at the basis of the third Positive Aging strategy: "you can use the past to cultivate wisdom." Wisdom, in this regard, is the skill of harnessing your past experiences to guide you in the present. The past as a source of wisdom can be construed using a map metaphor. Maps are guides that diagram terrain, roads, and geographic as well as political boundaries, based on previous surveying of the earth's surfaces. A traveler uses a map to plan routes through unknown areas. A map can be helpful in avoiding obstacles, barriers, or potential trouble that lie ahead. Like a map, the stream of experiences from the past holds information about life and can be accessed to assist us in life choices. If the past can be construed as a psychological road map, then it should help us efficiently navigate. However, unlike a road map, the signs and symbols embedded in the past are more difficult to discern for meaning. A past experience, for example, could hold a key source of knowledge for making a future decision, but this experience may be difficult to interpret because, unlike the universal symbols found on a geographical map, such an experience could carry different meaning for different people and across various circumstances. So reading a psychological map of your past is not as simple as interpreting a road map. But even the clearest road map or trail map is useless to the most skilled traveler unless it depicts the precise terrain through which one is moving. Our metaphorical map of the past may have an advantage in this regard, that is, past experiences are more flexible since they encompass an array of information that can ostensibly be applied to any new situation or circumstance.

In addition, experiences from the past often come in the form of templates (or sets) of knowledge that may be loosely tied to a specific situation or event. Like a geographical map, there must be some form of match between an experience template and a new situation. But, unlike a geographical map, experience templates are malleable and can be changed, adjusted, or even modified to have utility in addressing a present scenario. An individual who is good at identifying these experience templates and knows how to apply them in problem solving possesses a skill known as wisdom.

Since old age runs along the continuum of the life span where we have the greatest accumulation of experience the older we become, it is not surprising that skills subsumed under the umbrella of wisdom are more evident in later life. In Positive Aging, a building block for developing wisdom skills comes from how effectively we learn to link the past with the present and apply it to the future. Bridging these three dimensions of time is embodied in a life-span construct known as "Continuity." Theories of continuity have been promulgated by scholars and philosophers across history to help us understand how we adapt to our world and become wise.

This chapter provides a framework for how understanding the past and using the past promote wisdom. It is divided into three parts: Part I summarizes a contemporary formulation of how people cultivate continuity to connect the past, present, and future. Part II provides Positive Aging guidelines to help you learn to apply continuity theory to your ability to optimize your own aging process. You will learn here whether you are someone who seeks change and new experiences or whether your comfort is found in the security of sameness. Part III highlights issues that arise from too much change or too much sameness and how to reconcile these through Positive Aging principles.

Continuity Theory

The science of aging has been interested in the change-stability dynamic for some time. Since the 1960s, scholars in the field of adult life-span development have been writing about this construct and applying it to many situations and conditions of living (Aaronson, 1960; Crown & Heron, 1965; Erikson, Erikson, & Kivnick, 1986). In the 1980s Robert Atchely, a social psychologist, proposed a theory of aging based on ideas from his longitudinal research, which he called "continuity theory" (Atchley, 1999). Atchley's beliefs about continuity were formed from in-depth interviews with individuals who were 50 years and older participating in the Ohio Longitudinal Study of Aging and Adaptation (OLSAA), a population-based investigation of the older residents of a small town in middle America. Atchley investigated how people preserve their well-being and life satisfaction in the face of the deteriorative processes of aging that erode one's internal capacities and external resources, including the ending of important life roles like one's career and the loss of meaningful relationships. A remarkable aspect of this study was the resiliency of some of the OLSAA participants who weathered some disruptive and unanticipated changes in life circumstance that were due to many factors, including disease, loss of financial resources, and geographical moves. Atchley's research pinpointed that one source of their resiliency was their capacity to manage the sameness-change dialectic I described earlier. They took strength from predictable circumstances, but also found positive meaning in change. Atchley was interested in understanding the nature of this resilience and the ability of many of the OLSAA participants to maintain a stable sense of self even when old age created substantial barriers to everyday functioning. Atchley coined the term *continuity* to capture this striking intrapersonal resource.

Atchley argued that our identity in old age is influenced by enduring self-perceptions and life situations that shape how we view ourselves and others around us. It is this stable set of characteristics that are juxtaposed to age-related change that produce the dynamic that Atchley (1999) described in continuity theory:

> Despite significant changes in health, functioning, and social circumstances, a large proportion of older adults show considerable consistency over time in their patterns of thinking, activity profiles, living arrangements, and social relationships. (p. 1)

Continuity has value as a principle in Positive Aging because it was developed specifically with the older adult in mind. It is based on three constructs, two related to stability—"internal" and "external" continuity—and a third term that is descriptive of change, which he labeled "discontinuity." Atchley used this latter term, *discontinuity,* to mark a specific phenomenon that alters stability or the occurrence of a substantial shift in what is otherwise a routine life situation. Atchely posited that not all change is a discontinuity. Only when it disrupts or breaks the flow of an everyday life pattern is it a discontinuity. The distinction between discontinuity and change is described in more detail later. To set the stage, however, for formulating how Positive Agers use continuity to develop wisdom and resiliency the following is a description of each component of continuity theory.

Internal continuity is the consistent inner structure of your self, including your temperament or disposition, your emotional lability, and your energy level. It should be no surprise that if you ask someone who knows you well to describe you, it often fits your own sense of yourself. This is because others who are familiar with you have picked up on your patterns of thinking, feeling, and behaving, as these are the manifestations that make you a unique person. You might wonder whether it is possible to change how you present yourself to the world and if your traits get more resistant to change as you get older. In fact, one stereotype of old age that has persisted for generations is that people, as they age, become so singular in their outlook and behavior that it becomes a psychological entrenchment or internal prison from which a person cannot escape. Malcolm Cowley (1980) stated it this way:

> Even if the old are moderately cheerful . . . I suspect that most of them are haunted by fears that they prefer not to talk about. One of the fears . . . is that of declining into simplified versions of themselves, of being reduced from the complexity of adult life into a single characteristic. We have seen that happen to many persons in their last years. If they were habitually kind, in age they become . . . the image of benignity. . . . If they had always insisted on having their own way, in age they become masters or mistresses without servants. If they have always been dissatisfied, they become whiners and scolds. . . . Everything disappears from their personalities except one dominant trait. It is frightening to think that one might end as a caricature of oneself. (p. 56)

Everyone knows an older person who fits this stereotype. However, most people, as they get older, are not constrained to the degree of Cowley's caricature. His parody does highlight one way people cope with the changes and uncertainties of growing old, however, and that is to emphasize those features that tend to be rewarded and supported over time. Self-consistency can work to your benefit, in that cultivating stable qualities of acceptance, good will, and optimism can make life easier for you and help you to be more pleasant to live with. It can also work against you as well if you persist in rehearsing maladaptive routines, such as complaining and negativity. These then become an automatic part of your nature and your presentation to others. Either way, our inner self has something to gain in our remaining consistent over time. As Atchley (1999) related:

> I recently visited three older cousins of mine who knew me well when I was a teenager, but had not had any contact with me for nearly 30 years. They had no difficulty whatsoever identifying who I was and in relating to me. Their general mental models of who I was and what I was like were adapted

easily to include countless changes, including my career and family history. Many things had happened, but I was still basically the same Robert Atchley to them. I must say that I share their same view. Many of the basic inner patterns that constitute my unique self have remained relatively consistent even though over the years new inner perspectives have been added, and a great deal has changed in my external social circumstances. (p. 34)

External continuity involves the physical and social environment in which you live and the environment that you create for yourself that helps you feel meaningful. This involves your social roles, your relationships, where you live, and your activities. Atchley described external continuity in this way: "As a result of priority setting and selective investment throughout adulthood, by middle age most adults have unique and well-mapped external life situations or lifestyles that differentiate each person from others" (p. 10). These external indicators tell people what you value and how you prefer being recognized or acknowledged. Some scholars of life-span development have asserted that there is an interrelationship between our living environment and our personal dispositions. How we construct our roles and functions in society influences how we view ourselves and how we want others to view us (Lerner, 1986). Continuity theory suggests that we create and shape our own environment so it is more amenable to our internal sense of self—the clothes we wear, how we fix our hair, where we like to shop or eat, our favorite bar or coffee shop, brands of food that we prefer and so on. People notice when you change your pattern of dress or your hairstyle, your makeup, or even your weight because personal manifestations of external continuity are stable and represent who you are.

To explore factors that affect your external continuity, try this exercise. Look around your living space and notice features about it that appeal to you. Then think about a previous living arrangement. Note the features of your previous living space that have carried over into your current living situation. As you do this you will discover just how predictable you are in your choices and preferences.

On a larger social scale external continuity has influenced contemporary designs in geriatric residential living environments. These have shifted from one-size-fits-all industrial/institutionalized structures geared to 24-hour care needs (e.g., the nursing home) to less restrictive homelike settings that are more malleable to personal preferences and tastes, and help to preserve dignity and autonomy. In Australia, for example, the "home" concept is being pioneered by the Hammond Care Group, established in the 1930s, which is a not-for-profit, nondenominational faith-based organization specializing in care for older adults who do not have financial resources. Here are several principles in their design of long-term care facilities:

- Movement away from a large "common" room to additional smaller spaces for individual activities between staff, residents, and their families.
- A comfortable lounge area that is private for families to visit their loved one or a quiet area for staff to take individual residents or small groups for more personal conversations.
- A more pleasant main entrance that focuses on friendliness and invitation that accompanies most of the front entrances of a personal home. The entrance is a place to hang your hat and coat.
- Additional kitchen areas where relatives and friends are welcome to make tea or coffee without the assistance or supervision of staff and where residents can prepare meals with staff assistance.
- A garden area that is safe for residents to walk around in and an opportunity for residents to grow plants and garden vegetables if they are able.
- A functional laundry room where residents can wash clothes.
- An infrastructure (e.g., nurse's station) that is hidden from resident view, but allows staff to move into and out of the facility to provide services while at the same time being unobtrusive to residents.

These guidelines are examples of 21st century ways of thinking and planning about long-term care that incorporate principles of continuity. Working to make a care environment more homelike applies external continuity principles and, in the long run, will be more cost-efficient because it preserves independence and dignity.

In the United States similar efforts are under way that emphasize graded levels of services that increase as care needs to become more substantial. A "levels of care—stages of decline" model (Thorn, 2002) is captured in Figure 3.1.

50

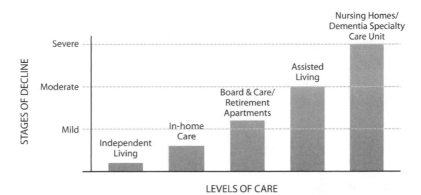

FIGURE 3.1. CARE NEEDS INCREASE AS COGNITIVE FUNCTION AND HEALTH DECLINE.

This model involves matching the level of care provided with the current and future needs of the individual. In early or mild stages of decline fewer services are required to meet the needs of older people who wish to remain as independent and self-sufficient as possible. When physical or cognitive decline advances to moderate and severe stages, direct assistance with daily living tasks and professional services (such as medical, nursing, and mental health care) are needed. These constitute a higher level of care. Assisted living facilities can often meet the needs of people with moderate levels of decline, whereas skilled nursing facilities are appropriate for those with more severe medical needs. Specialized dementia (or Alzheimer's disease) care units are providing innovative residential care for people who suffer from severe cognitive deficits due to these disease states.

There is promise in a "levels-of-care" approach, not only in making care mirror everyday living, but as a way to reduce care costs by relying on an older person to continue to use his or her capacities for independent living for as long as possible, thereby reducing the costs associated with skilled professionals providing assistance with everyday living and personal self-care.

On a smaller scale, an intriguing manifestation of external continuity is embodied in an idea known as the "memory box" (Hill & Gregg, 2002). This is a contemporary strategy used by residential care settings to facilitate continuity when moving from independent to assisted care living. A memory box is no more than a wall display case where older residents can place items including pictures, awards, jewelry, and other memorabilia of life significance to help them sustain continuity as they move from their homes into residential care. Studies have found that the memory box technique promotes better adjustment and life satisfaction by helping residents remain connected to their "sense of self."

Regardless of your context, and even in age-related decline, as you work to preserve your dignity you cultivate maturity. Introduced in Chapter 1, maturation is a positive manifestation of age-related decline. At its most fundamental level, maturation is a form of learning that involves getting better at living by learning through experience. Whether good or bad, experiences teach us that we can change and adapt to our situation and circumstances. Those who are good at this are mature.

Maturation can be gauged by how well we apply Positive Aging principles in everyday living. The simple accumulating of years of living is not the singular condition that produces maturation. Some people who are old enough to collect social security checks have never evolved beyond their adolescent years. Those who are unable to learn from experience will become more entrenched in their ways as a function of aging and are at risk of becoming living examples of old-age rigidity.

I recall an elderly neighbor who had lived on our street for many years. For most of these years, the exit street from our housing complex involved driving to the end of the road and making a right turn out. As the housing complex grew, a second neighborhood was built on the right-hand side of the road, blocking this exit street. A new exit was constructed that required driving a few feet past the right-hand exit, then taking a left-hand turn, then looping around the complex to exit on the main road. My elderly neighbor had great trouble with this change. Each time he passed the right-hand turn-out he would hit his signal bar to engage the right blinker. He would then unconsciously start into the turn, but would stop short when he realized that the turn was no longer there. He repeated this behavior day after day and it began to infuriate him. His wife and children noticed his error, as did his other neighbors. He said to me on one occasion, "I've practiced this routine for such a long time that it simply won't go away. I've even put a taped arrow pointing left on my dashboard to remind me that the turn is no longer there. This has helped a little, but my family makes fun of my painted-arrow dashboard." My neighbor's ingrained pattern persisted even though his context and family were pushing him to change. It brings to mind the adage, "Old habits die hard."

We act and behave in certain ways because of the forces of internal and external continuity. Our propensity to repeat behaviors is adaptive because it creates predictability. Patterns are something we can count on. On the other hand, the world is a dynamic place and we must change and adjust ourselves and our circumstances if we want to adapt. Learning, described in Chapter 2, is a Positive Aging strategy that can be used to challenge the forces of continuity when they are no longer adaptive. The ability to cultivate flexibility over time through learning and applying new information is Positive Aging in action.

Discontinuity is a source of change that disrupts stability. It is change that diminishes the capacity for coherence with respect to internal or external continuity. If I am in the habit of putting my car keys in a dish on my dresser each evening before I go to bed, when I wake up the next morning I expect that they will still be in their place. When this occurs it represents external continuity. My keys are where I put them. If the next morning my keys are not where I thought I placed them, then I wonder where they might be. I am mildly distressed. Unless I find my keys, I will miss an appointment and my day-to-day routine will be disrupted. I might ask myself, "Where did those keys go? Is it possible that someone took them? Is it possible that I misplaced them the night before?" I am now in the situation of trying to recall what I did the previous day when I had my keys. I engage in this behavior because I am trying to generate clues that are at the root of why a regular routine has broken down. Misplacing keys is a small discontinuity, but there are large ones as well that can permanently disrupt your life routine, including the loss of a spouse, moving to a new home, or even winning a major prize. Whether large or small, positive or negative, discontinuities cause us to change. They are an essential feature of the life-span architecture. They shape who we are and how we go through life.

There are several consequences of discontinuity. First, when it occurs, we usually notice it. Discontinuities cause us to stop, pause, and reflect on where we are and where we are headed. Second, a discontinuity immediately focuses us on the present. We are in the moment, even if it is for a brief period of time. Sometimes a discontinuity can be so large that it will disrupt us for some time, and for these, we may need psychological tools to reestablish our life routine.

Atul Gawande (2007) described Felix Silverstone, a well-known geriatrician with a discontinuity:

> He [Felix] is 87 years old . . . and at 82 he had to retire. The problem wasn't his health; it was that of his wife, Bella. Felix no longer felt safe leaving her home alone, and in 2001 he gave up his practice. They moved to Orchard Cove, a retirement community . . . where they could be closer to their sons. "I didn't think I would survive the change," Felix said. He'd observed in his patients how difficult the transitions of age could be. Examining his last patient, packing up his home, he felt that he was about to die. "I was taking apart my life as well as the house," he recalled. "It was terrible." (p. 57).

For Felix, discontinuities associated with retirement from his medical practice and moving to an assisted living community—even though they were necessary—were life-changing discontinuities that had a profound effect on him. A critical feature of this story is that he moved near his sons, who helped him to reestablish his equilibrium and restore his sense of stability. This discontinuity made him appreciate what it meant to be "elderly." Even in his very advanced age, this experience was a source of maturation and learning.

II. POSITIVE AGING AND CONTINUITY

Although it may sometimes seem that life has no real purpose or meaning, and that we can't control our experiences, Malcolm Cowley (1980) argued otherwise:

> One project among many, one that tempts me and might be tempting to others, is trying to find a shape or pattern in our lives. There are such patterns, I believe, even if they are hard to discern. Our lives that seemed a random and monotonous series of incidents are something more than that; each of them has a plot. . . . Can we clear away the bundles of old newspapers, evading the booby traps, and lay bare the outlines

of ourselves? Those outlines, if we find them, will prove to be a story, one with a beginning, a development, a climax . . . and an epilogue. . . . In age we have the privilege—which sometimes becomes a torture on sleepless nights—of passing judgment on our own performance. But before passing judgment, we have to untangle the plot of the play. (pp. 70–72)

The older we get the more recognizable our patterns of behavior become, and we learn what we do to preserve continuity. This understanding is an essential aspect of Positive Aging. We are predictable because our stable internal continuity shapes our regular patterns of behavior. In turn, our behaviors then influence how we feel about ourselves. Most of us preserve continuity in good times and bad, but when life throws us a challenge we must rely on skills to reestablish continuity, and this is where Positive Aging comes in.

Positive Aging makes continuity theory active by employing a life-span stylistic for dealing with change by approaching tasks in a way to optimize our own well-being. We do this through employing the four Positive Aging characteristics: mobilizing resources, making affirmative life choices, cultivating flexibility, and focusing on the positives. These work as methods for cultivating wisdom in old age.

Mobilizing Your Resources

We all possess assets that we employ to help us in living and in coping with life's challenges. How these are accessed to enhance learning and meaning in later life can be highly personal, but there are some common elements in mobilizing resources. Accessing your resources can be challenging when you are experiencing a crisis, so being aware of how to activate resources beforehand may be helpful. One method that is frequently used by Positive Agers is reflecting on past experiences or times when you used your resources wisely. It is possible that the way you addressed an earlier problem might be useful if it is modified to fit a present concern. The goal is to harness experiences from the past to solve present problems. Following is an example that illustrates this.

SUSIE AND LIST MAKING

Susie, who is 87 years old, has a big decision to make—whether to sell her home that she has lived in for 60 years and move to an assisted living facility, or stay where she is for the time being. This issue surfaced the previous year when she started having problems with arthritis that made getting around her large home and yard and taking care of herself difficult. She has been experiencing increased difficulties preparing meals and doing household chores, but she is still able to take care of herself, including bathing, getting dressed, and moving from her bed to her living room. Her children are encouraging a move because they do not live close to Susie and are only able to help her occasionally. None of her children are in a position to move into Susie's home and to help her on a day-to-day basis. Susie has also been experiencing some loneliness. Having been a widow for seven years, she has learned to get along without her husband, but she is starting to miss companionship. Since she doesn't drive, it is becoming harder to get out and meet people or attend neighborhood and community activities.

Susie recalled that when she and her husband were looking to purchase this home, they had several options they were considering. To help them choose they made a list of the characteristics and the pros and cons of each home, including cost, location, floor plan, schools, and so on. At that time it proved to be an effective tool in making the decision of which house to purchase. From time to time they would wonder whether this house was the right choice, but then they would remember the list and be reassured about their decision.

Interestingly, Susie was reminded about the home-buying list when her friend visited and suggested that she make a list of the benefits and the downsides she might experience if she chose to move to the assisted living center. Susie made this list:

Pros for staying in my home.
- *I'm familiar with it.*
- *My children know where I am.*
- *I have friends and family who live close by.*

Cons for staying in my home.
- *I keep bumping into things and having minor accidents when I move around my home.*
- *I am lonely living here by myself.*
- *I am afraid that someone might break in and hurt me.*
- *I can't take out the garbage without help.*

- *I keep forgetting to do things like turn lights off, lock doors, turn the stove off. I might cause a fire in my sleep.*

Pros for going to Garden Terrace Assisted Living.

- *I like the area.*
- *My kids think I will feel more comfortable.*
- *I wouldn't have to fix my own meals.*
- *I could still come and go and could have access to transportation to doctors, my hair stylist, my book group, through the facility.*

Cons for going to Garden Terrace Assisted Living.

- *It's very expensive.*
- *I don't like the idea of living in a facility.*
- *I like my independence.*
- *I'm not comfortable being around a lot of people.*
- *My kids might forget about me if I live there.*

Susie's list involves several important features. Her list includes things she values and her beliefs about the positives and negatives of staying or moving that affect her. As she works on her list she will identify issues that are important to her in making this decision. She can then follow up on these issues. For example, she fears that if she moves into Garden Terrace, her kids will forget about her. By putting this issue on her list, she not only acknowledges it, but now she has permission to talk with her kids about this and get their viewpoints about how they would continue to stay in touch with their mom if she is in this facility.

Lists can be helpful in clarifying some decisions, such as the one described for Susie. However, when decisions are more complex, particularly those that involve medical concerns, multiple issues may need to be considered. Some medical decisions are so complex that strategies have been promulgated that can aid in decision making. One model specific to making medical decisions in later life is the Ottawa Personal Decision Guide (2004, available at http://decisionaid. ohri.ca/decguide.html). This guide contains a comprehensive list of factors to consider before making a decision and describes the following key steps: (1) clarifying the issue; (2) identifying your resources; (3) approaching decisions flexibly and keeping your options open; and (4) committing to knowing that you have made the best choice under the circumstances. These steps contain elements of the characteristics of Positive Aging. Let us apply these steps to a hypothetical situation, in which you begin to notice that your life partner or spouse is experiencing progressively worsening memory problems. You feel that you must make some decisions regarding this situation and you need to develop a plan. Your plan could involve the four steps as follows.

The first step is to clarify the issue. How much do you know about memory problems? What are the signs that memory problems are not just normal forgetting? How would you know if these problems are the symptoms of a disease? To explore these questions, you might seek answers from various professionals such as your personal physician, or you might consult the Internet. As you engage in this learning process, you will likely take your loved one to a clinic where he or she can be tested for memory impairment. If your concerns are warranted, this will trigger more decision making. Faced with such a dilemma, you might wonder whether you have the where-with-all to deal with such difficult decisions, such as deciding whether to move to be nearer necessary medical care, whether to employ outside help, and how to deal with the financial impact of any necessary medical procedures. It is important to remain optimistic at this juncture, and it is helpful to focus on decision needs as they arise, and not get too caught up in speculating about the long-term. You probably do have the resources to deal with issues in the present.

The second step is to assess your personal assets, including how much you can rely on your partner to be an equal participant in the decision-making process. You will want to define your personal, financial, and social resources, that is, those resources that you have immediately available to you, as well as resources that you may need to tap in the future (such as help from children, extended family and others).

The third step is to remain flexible and keep your options open. Gathering more information may open the door to options that you would not consider otherwise. Being open to possibilities as your situation unfolds does not mean that you are apprehensive. On the contrary, it suggests that you are working to make the best decisions as needs arise in the presence of changing circumstances. You will make many decisions as the process unfolds and staying flexible, but at the same time hopeful, will help you along the way.

The fourth step involves committing to your decisions. You may be asked to help your partner start a medication regimen involving drugs that have challenging side effects. In this instance, taking medication may make your partner sick; however, if the goal is to preserve memory function, then committing to helping your partner take her or his medicine is important. Commitment does limit your options, because once you set your course down a pathway it is critical to stay on that course. This does not mean that you should not re-evaluate a decision from time to time, but moving forward is important in this final stage if you want to make progress towards a desired outcome— in this case, helping your partner deal with a memory impairment and preserving your sense of well-being in the process.

Not all decisions require elaborate steps like those described above. In fact, we make many decisions in a single day that involve only thinking through the issue or problem and choosing the best course of action. However, when it comes to more significant decisions that involve an expenditure of time and emotional resources and contain an element of risk, then a more formal strategy for making such decisions can be useful.

One significant decision we all must make is what to do with our money and tangible assets as we become old and die. List making or decision guides can be useful tools in estate planning. There are other areas in our lives in which lists can be useful such as dealing with the disablement process. Strategies and approaches to making decisions are needed if we are to efficiently mobilize our resources and be Positive Agers.

Making Life Choices That Promote Wisdom

Our life situation is partly a reflection of the choices that we make over time. The longer we live, the more choices we make, which then sets in motion a life pattern due to such choices. This is, perhaps, the most compelling feature of continuity. If you think about it, you are making decisions all the time, many of which you are unaware. Once a life pattern is set in place, then decisions and choices from that pattern can be made with very little resource utilization. This is why life patterns are attractive; they reduce our need to be consciously aware of what we are doing all the time. The problem arises when we set in motion a life choice that is maladaptive, as is highlighted in the following example.

MIKE'S CHALLENGE

Mike is 60 years old and has held a number of jobs over the course of his life. In his youth, Mike attended college. After six years he earned a bachelor's degree in interdisciplinary studies. He had trouble at the time choosing a major, so he decided that graduating was more important than defining an area of focus. Mike was married for two years in his 20s but when this marriage failed, he was never able to fully engage in a new relationship. This was perplexing to him because he believed that he should have a life partner and he yearned for this experience. He had gotten close to marrying several women who were younger than he, but he reported, "As these relationships got more involved and we would start discussing marriage, things would become ambiguous and the relationship would deteriorate." At 60, Mike felt that his life would not be complete unless he got married soon. At the gym he regularly attended, he shared these concerns with his trainer who was in his 40s and had never been married. His trainer listened to Mike and suggested that after Mike's first failed marriage, Mike had made a lifestyle choice to be single and had simply set that lifestyle choice in place through his subsequent behaviors. The only problem was that Mike didn't realize that he had made this decision. The trainer suggested that Mike look closely at his life; Mike's selection of friends, his choice to live in an apartment downtown, and his habits all argued for single living. And Mike liked his carefree lifestyle and enjoyed the support from his extended family that he had managed to acquire across his adult life span. Mike thought about this for some time and struggled with the idea. He subsequently sought counseling and his presenting problem to the counselor was: "I'm 60 years old, am not married, and am terrified to die alone." After meeting with the counselor for multiple sessions, the counselor reframed Mike's problem as "discomfort with his lifestyle choice to live as a single person."

Mike had made a lifestyle choice without being fully aware of it, and both his trainer and counselor had identified it. The issue was not whether Mike was married or not, it was really whether Mike wanted to move forward with his choice to be a single person, affirm this lifestyle choice, and then work to reconcile inconsistencies associated with that choice. Mike has a well-paying job, owns a downtown apartment, and has many social relationships. Does he want to give up his lifestyle? It may be that Mike does want to change; however, it is also possible that his life can be full and complete as he affirms his current choice and then focuses on how to get the most out of life and his old age as a single person. Either way, understanding the bigger picture related to lifestyle will help Mike be happier and more content with his situation.

Cultivating Flexibility

How does flexibility sustain a stable routine or pattern that has value but is difficult to maintain because of its high level of sameness? This question has been asked by employees who watch the clock tick down as boredom makes ending the shift more and more difficult. The example of a toll-booth operator comes to mind. Here is a person who, day in and day out, collects tolls. For each traveler, the task is the same, and each step in the toll-booth collector's job is highly routine: stick out your hand, take the money, put it in the cash register, raise the toll bar, let the car go through, lower the toll bar, wave the next car forward, stick out your hand, and so forth. For most of us looking from the outside, toll collecting is a means-to-an-end job. But how might one deal with the repetitive nature of this job? One way could be to use strategies that build variation or flexibility into the job by emphasizing different aspects of it. For example, although travelers are encouraged to provide exact change, this may not always occur. Sometimes the toll booth operator will be handed a $5 bill and then a new behavior is required: making the correct change. Perhaps there are other ways to make the job more interesting (noting the state on the license plates, keeping track of the gender of travelers). These strategies will not only maintain interest, but could help the toll booth operator remain vigilant and mentally active across the course of a workday. In any case, the person who will find satisfaction in the job and do it well will find ways to create flexibility in this context.

This example demonstrates how flexibility can make even the tedious tolerable; however, the role of flexibility as a Positive Aging strategy for finding wisdom in old age is large. Past experiences do not always precisely fit a current situation or problem. The situation may require modifying a past experience to make it work for you in the present. In the example of Susie's list, she recalls using a listing strategy in the past, but to make it work for her current issue, she needs to modify it, including the categories on the list. This requires flexibility. It is important to note that flexibility also involves some risk. To modify an experience or to think about something in a different way may create a whole range of possibilities for addressing a problem or situation. Some ideas may not work as well as others, so in addition to cultivating flexibility, one needs to develop strategies for ranking or rating choices based on how well they will work in a given situation. The best way to do this is to be willing to try new things and then evaluate how useful they were, even when some options may set you back from time to time. This requires that you not only be careful in how you make new choices, but that you have a degree of compassion for yourself when you make an errant choice.

Developing flexibility, then, does not come without work, effort, and practice, and even failure once in a while. However, the more you practice stepping back, weighing all of your options, and probing for that new direction or way that may help you solve a situation or issue, the better you will become at being flexible and the closer you will get to attaining wisdom.

Emphasizing the Positives

For better or worse, life situations change as you age; you may discover newfound freedom in retirement, a medical test could reveal a chronic health problem, a family member might die, a new grandchild could come into your life, you could no longer see well enough to drive your car even with glasses, or you might cultivate a new hobby. Such a list of positives and negatives exists for every person and both lists expand the longer you live. What is interesting in this regard is that people tend to focus on one list or the other. It is rare that a person can look at both pros and cons from a neutral perspective. To be a Positive Ager, however, it is essential to acknowledge both the positives and negatives in life while at the same time emphasizing the positive. This does not mean that you should ignore the negative because there are lessons to be learned from life's difficulties and they reinforce meaning in the positive (e.g., the loss of a significant other may make more meaningful those relationships that remain).

People who develop a habit of emphasizing the positive do better when they are confronted with challenges or difficulties in life. A life-span manifestation of emphasizing the positives is optimism. A person who is optimistic looks for the positive and then affirms aspects of the situation or oneself that can be counted on to generate positive emotions even when the situation is difficult. Such an approach has the consequence of enabling resources that can then reinstate continuity. Is it possible to cultivate or learn optimism? The answer to this question is yes. In fact, in Positive Aging everyone has the capability to be happy in old age. All that is required is that you discipline yourself to reframe perceptions and cultivate positive emotions as you cope with the dilemmas of late-life living. The following example highlights how this can be done:

STEVE'S VIEWPOINT

Sixty-seven-year-old Steve had a number of challenges in his life. He was a combat veteran wounded in the Vietnam War. He had been in the trajectory of a land mine and shrapnel was embedded in his neck, which damaged his vocal cords. The damage was permanent and his voice was reduced to a whisper. At the time, there were few surgical fixes for his problem, but there were prosthetic devices that could amplify his voice. He elected not to use these, so he moved forward in life with this speech impediment. At first he was embarrassed by it. In fact, he became quite introverted as a way to cope with this impairment. He became reclusive and began to drink alcohol heavily. This behavior persisted for nearly a decade until Steve felt that his life was unbearable. His sister, who was concerned about his health, suggested that he try to change his viewpoint. Steve laughed at this and referred her back to his combat-related disability. She, however, challenged Steve and said that he could not change his voice, but he could change his drinking. Steve decided to attend Alcoholics Anonymous meetings. He was struck by the people in these meetings who were able to "kick" the habit. They all had hard-luck situations, but those who turned their drinking around turned around their attitudes as well. It seemed to him that they had made the conscious decision to think and speak positively, regardless of their situation. So, Steve set up a plan. He bought a counter and kept track during the week of every negative statement he made (he did not count his thoughts, only his verbal utterances). He then started decreasing these verbalizations by half each month. This allowed him to still say a negative thing or two, but the focus of his conversations would slowly turn to the positive. He meticulously engaged this plan and started feeling better. He had a setback now and again, but his positive verbalizations seemed to give him energy to stay off alcohol, interact with other people, and start making plans for his future. He began going to a local coffee shop. There he met a group of older retired men who were regulars at the senior center and they invited him to join them for cards. At first Steve felt embarrassed to attend, but these friends seemed not to care about his whispered speech. In fact one said, "Your quiet speech could serve you in card playing by making it harder for others to guess your hand." Steve liked this rationale and he liked playing cards, so he started going and became a regular at the card table. He also went on a few trips to Las Vegas with his friends and enjoyed playing poker at tables there. He got to be quite an expert. His sister was amazed and she asked Steve how he did it. Steve indicated that he just got tired of feeling sorry for himself and decided to take life "by the horns" and make it work.

III. POSITIVE AGING: THE PATHWAY TO WISDOM

Larger-than-life historical and/or religious figures have demonstrated an extraordinary capacity for wisdom in managing difficult life events. King Solomon, for example, a biblical figure considered to possess great wisdom, was characterized in this way because he helped people under his rule address important life issues. His method of arbitration involved actualizing the intrinsic good in people in order to arrive at a worthwhile solution for all. The following oft-told story is paraphrased as an exemplar of this kind of wisdom.

> Two women come to King Solomon looking for justice. Each had an infant, but by virtue of an accident one of the women had suffocated her child and had switched her dead baby with the other woman's living baby. Both now claimed the living infant was theirs. Solomon addressed the conflicting claims of these women in the following way: He ordered that a sword be brought to the court and offered to give each woman half of the disputed child. As he had hoped, the real mother revealed herself when she relinquished her claim in order to spare the child's life. (1 Kings 3–4)

In line with continuity theory, it may be that Solomon employed this strategy based on a broad knowledge base acquired over a life span of learning. In this regard, wisdom as a life-span skill capitalizes on the interplay of maturational processes and lifelong learning in promoting a way of relating and acting on the world that promotes a greater understanding of the complexity and uncertainties of life.

Positive Aging represents a lifestyle which produces a "wise" skill set. Unlike the pessimistic view of age-related decline, wisdom seems to improve as one becomes older. In many respects, wisdom is enhanced by the ability to learn from life experience and to make more effective life decisions.

Given that wisdom is considered by researchers and scholars to have components that are tied to skill acquisition across the life span, the question arises as to whether there are strategies or suggestions that can help a person learn how to be wise. Although wisdom is often developed by creating meaning from ambiguity, there are several features that are characteristic of wise people. These features are listed in terms of how one might develop such qualities:

- Be orientated toward others.
  - Be open and willing to teach others.
  - Help those who are less fortunate.
- Learn from your mistakes.
  - Be careful to avoid the pitfalls of cycles that are evident from the past.
- Practice integrating information.
  - Study a problem from many different perspectives.
- Be reflective about issues and problems.
  - Avoid choosing the first solution that enters your mind.
  - Be willing to wrestle with ambiguity in order to find meaning in it.
  - The speed of problem solving may not be the best marker of wisdom. "Leaders are decisive, wise people are reflective."
- Cultivate optimism.
  - Be positive about yourself and others.
  - Realize the world is not a perfect place and that bad things happen and cannot be always avoided.

- Focus on the positives to ameliorate aspects of negative life events.

It is clear from the scientific and philosophical literature that an essential ingredient in wisdom is life experience. This concept has been echoed throughout the ages. In his well-known book *Modern Man in Search of a Soul* Carl Jung (1933), one of the most influential thinkers of self-psychology in our modern-day era and founder of analytical psychology, wrote:

> A human being would certainly not grow to be seventy or eighty years old if this longevity had no meaning for the species to which he belonged. (p. 787)

This quote underscores the truism that the longer we live, the more we can learn. Some have suggested that it takes over 60 years to learn how to "live one's life." Positive Aging facilitates learning and the use of knowledge as strategies to enhance old age and provide important information about the nature of living. If one outcome of Positive Aging is the emergence of wisdom, then from a developmental point of view the earlier one can utilize the strategies of Positive Aging, the more likely it will be that it will not only promote well-being and life satisfaction for the learner, but it can be taught to future generations. Maximum life span is longer than ever before, but it is still time limited. Learning how to live and prosper in the space of that age span represents one of the most significant personal and social opportunities of the 21st century.

Chapter 4

STRATEGY #4: YOU CAN STRENGTHEN LIFE-SPAN RELATIONSHIPS

I. THE NEED TO BELONG

You belong. Although there are times when you might feel that you don't, if you think about your situation you will discover others who are interested in you and in your well-being. This may be your family; you may live with a spouse or a partner or you may have children. If you have no children or partner, you may have relatives either distant or close. If you have no extended family, you may have friends, neighbors, or caregivers with whom you are connected. Perhaps you have indirect connections with others by listening to the radio or watching television or even through the Internet.

If most of us belong to someone or are part of some group, then why do people feel lonely? This question raises the important issue of the need to belong. The need to belong is an emotion or a desire to be a part of someone's life; to be connected to others in some way. Researchers suggest that the need to belong is not only influenced by how many people you know, but is a subjective state that is affected by your mood, your health, and your self-perceptions. People who suffer from a depressed mood may feel like they don't belong, even if they are surrounded by supportive family or loved ones. Science has discovered that the need to belong persists across the life span and that it is not the same for all people (Baumeister & Twenge, 2003). Some individuals have a high need to belong and may feel lonely even if they are surrounded by others. There are those who have less of a need to belong and may be content with their social relations even though they have few personal connections (Stevens, Martina, & Westerhof, 2006).

As a life-span construct, the need to belong can also involve specific behaviors. These are:

- Interaction
- Concern
- Caring

This interaction-concern-caring triad has received substantial attention in the adult life-span literature as a way to explain the forces that influence one's inner sense that one is connected to others in a meaningful way (Baumeister & Leary, 1995). Interaction is a label for social exchange. This could be as simple as a greeting from a neighbor, or a brief conversation with your grocer or hair stylist. Interaction could involve a group of people who enjoy playing pinochle together. Concern involves interaction that includes an expression of awareness about your needs. A friend who shows sympathy when he or she becomes aware that you have experienced a loss is an example of a display of concern. Caring is showing not only a deeper understanding of another person's situation, but also expressing a willingness to help as needed. When you care about another person you want to help that person in a meaningful way. In return, the person you care about will likely want to help you. Caring can be found between intimate life partners, children and parents, and others with whom you feel a close bond.

How does this triad of belonging behaviors work in your own life? Take your neighbors as an example. You might live on a street where you have many neighbors. While it may be comforting to know that your neighbors are available if there were a catastrophe, just being aware of your neighbors will not usually fill your need to belong unless you *interact* with them. When there is interaction between you and a neighbor, several things happen. First, you get to know your neighbor; you learn your neighbor's name. Let's say her name is Karen. When you interact with Karen, you learn something about her. Karen learns something about you as well. Karen shows *concern* for you by asking about your welfare. Showing concern implies that you are interested in another person's issues and needs. You may reciprocate that concern by inquiring about Karen's welfare. Expressed concern deepens relationships, but only expressing concern will not foster lasting relationship bonds. This happens when you extend yourself by acting in such a way that offers help. Let's say that your garden needs weeding, but you are having trouble with arthritis and are no longer able to do the weeding yourself. Karen may offer to help you weed your garden and as she does so, she shows *caring*. This example of interaction, concern, and caring highlights how the give-and-take process of the triad of belonging behaviors nurtures relationships, including encouraging you and Karen to feel like you belong to each other. In fact, as this relationship develops, your notion of "neighbors" may move from passive awareness to actively counting on neighbors like Karen as resources for filling needs, especially your need to belong.

In this example Karen is active; she initiates the neighbor relationship, she shows concern, and she cares about you. Another neighbor, let's say John, lives across the street but doesn't interact much with you. Although he waves hello when he sees you, John never ventures across the street. By his "staying away," your relationship with John does not deepen. At first, you might wave back, but after a while you may tire of even this superficial interchange. It doesn't fill your need to belong. Here, you have only the interaction behavior, and although it does initially influence your need to belong, you might still feel lonely even though John waves to you each time he sees you outside.

The example of John underscores that meeting the "need to belong" is reciprocal. Even if another person initiates a relationship, the receiver must also respond in kind and, where possible, move the relationship forward. If John waves from across the street and then you walk over and start visiting with him, then the relationship might progress. Of course John would need to reciprocate your gesture by showing some interest in you. This give-and-take in relationships is what strengthens them and makes them more meaningful. If you think about the many people you know or have some connection to, you will discover that the more important relationships involve all three of the belonging behaviors. The following exercise will help you understand how this dynamic works in your own life:

BELONGING EXERCISE

Think of an important person in you life.
- Does this person show all three belonging behaviors?
- How do *you* show interaction, concern, and caring in this relationship?

Think of someone who you know, but don't feel particularly attached to.
- How do belonging behaviors manifest themselves (or fail to show themselves) in this relationship?

Identify an existing relationship that you want to enhance.
- How might you enhance your interactions with this person?
- How might you show concern?
- How might you show caring?
- Try to act on one of these belonging behaviors and observe how this relationship changes in response to your actions.

It is also not necessary to be physically present to belong. The image of the "pen pal" comes to mind. Corresponding through letters, interacting on the telephone, sending and receiving e-mails, and chatting on the Internet are all mediums through which belonging can occur. In these instances it is clear that interaction occurs, but what about the other two belonging behaviors, concern and caring? Can a person show these over the phone or through the Internet? The following story illustrates how this might be done:

MARTHA'S FALL

Martha was a very social person even in her 80s. She was very involved in neighborhood activities even after her husband passed away several years earlier. One activity that Martha placed high value on was her membership in a book group that had met monthly for 7 years. Composed mostly of neighbors who had common reading interests, Martha had led many of these groups and had been instrumental in selecting many of the reading lists for the group. On an icy morning

Martha slipped on her front porch and broke her hip. She also suffered a concussion that precipitated some memory loss and disturbance in her vision. After this accident, she had difficulty getting around and was no longer motivated to attend the book group. She was absent for many months. One of her close friends, Evelyn, who was 20 years younger, noticed Martha's absence from the group and went over to Martha's home and visited with her. Evelyn learned that Martha was still interested in the book group, but did not feel physically comfortable sitting through the meetings and was embarrassed that she was not able to read like she used to. Evelyn suggested that if Martha still wanted to be part of the group, Evelyn could meet with Martha monthly and share with her the group discussions about the books that were being read. Evelyn even said that she would read to Martha if Martha was not able to see clearly. Martha liked the idea and Evelyn began coming over monthly. Martha set up an Internet connection so that Evelyn could send materials from the book group and Martha could participate in real-time with the group. Evelyn helped Martha get some of the books that were available in an electronic format and listen to them over the computer speakers. Through this process Martha was able to participate with the book group and her relationships with Evelyn deepened.

In this story, Martha found herself unable to participate in the book group in the way that she was accustomed to. The book club had been a way that she was nurturing her sense of belonging in the community. After her fall, Martha's sense of connection was severed. However, with the help of a member of the book group, Martha recaptured her feeling of belonging, although in a somewhat different way. Now, it was through Evelyn's assistance and by employing the Internet and computer. Evelyn showed concern, and then caring for Martha. She took the time to keep Martha connected, including reading to her and giving her materials from the group. The relationship between Evelyn and Martha became more meaningful as they continued to meet.

Research indicates that although a person's need to belong is a stable trait, changes in one's social circles will inevitably occur over time. Antonucci, a gerontologist who studied social support in old age, coined the term *social convoy* to characterize the various relationships in one's life (Antonucci & Akiyama, 1987). Figure 4.1 is an example of a social convoy. The center or the bull's-eye in this diagram is "you."

Outward from "you" there are three rings that form concentric circles which describe the kinds of relationships you may have. The outermost ring is labeled *interaction*, to identify those people who would meet only the most superficial level of belonging. This ring includes casual relationships like the example of John, your neighbor who waves from across the street. The other people in this ring might include coworkers, or people you might encounter in your day-to-day travels and who interact with you around limited issues, like the bank teller, your pharmacist, or someone you meet and visit with once in a while at the grocery store. These are people who may or may not be interested in you. If they are interested, it is usually confined to the activity or to the task that you are engaged in at the time, such as completing a project with a colleague at work, or an occasional appointment with your hair stylist or barber.

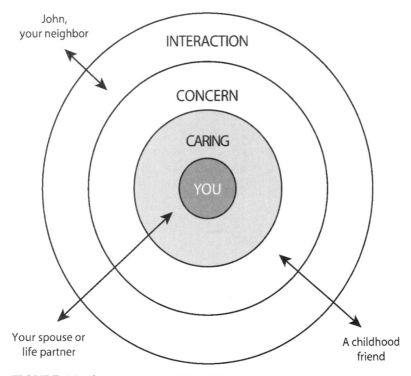

FIGURE 4.1. A SOCIAL CONVOY MODEL.

The next circle represents those people who have not only interacted with you, but who have expressed concern about your welfare and in whom you are interested. These people are more familiar to you and you know more about them. This may be a childhood friend with whom you have regularly exchanged holiday cards, or a member of the senior center which you have attended regularly, or a neighbor with whom you've had frequent interactions over the years, or even a distant relative whom you have seen once or twice a year. Finally, the innermost circle that borders the bull's-eye "you" represents people who not only interact and are concerned about you, but who *care* about you as well. These are family members, close relatives, your life partner, or your best friend. These are highly meaningful people who have directly met your need to belong in the past and who are sources of support for you in the present and in the future. They are there when you need them. In most instances, the people in this inner circle are individuals who have engaged with you in the triad of belonging behaviors, "interaction-concern-caring."

The social convoy is a tool you can use to think about your different relationships. Try the following exercise.

EXERCISE: CREATING YOUR SOCIAL CONVOY

Figure 4.2 on the next page is a diagram of a social convoy model with spaces or blanks where you can fill in people you know who represent each of these categories. As you engage in this exercise, you will begin to appreciate how important that inner circle is to your well-being.

People, of course, vary in the number of persons that they can list in the various circles, and your diagram can be used to get a sense of how you view people in your life in relation to your sense of belonging. An important feature of the social convoy is that it also predicts how change occurs in the number and composition of your social network; the inner circle is the most stable and it is likely that you are highly motivated to stay connected to these people even if they are physically distant from you. If you were to complete this social convoy model on a yearly basis, you would notice that people in your inner circle tend to be stable while those in the outer circles change more frequently.

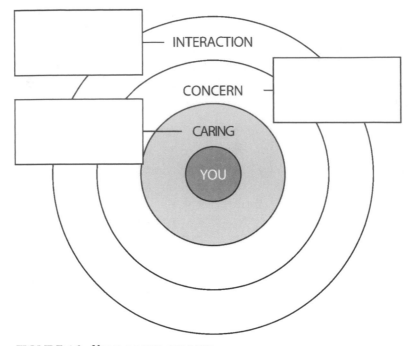

FIGURE 4.2. YOUR SOCIAL CONVOY.

II. POSITIVE AGING AND BELONGING

Applying Positive Aging characteristics to build relationships in later life can fill your need to belong. The old adage that you must "be a friend to have a friend" applies here because it acknowledges that relationship building is a two-way street; whether you are old or young, the same formula applies. You must give and receive to strengthen relationships; put in the terms of science, the reciprocity of expressed interest, concern, and caring is a prerequisite to meaningful life-span relationships. How this occurs may be different in old age than at other times in the life cycle, but even if you are homebound or are suffering from a chronic illness that makes contact with others difficult, those about whom you deeply care will find ways to remain connected to sustain belonging. Positive Agers know how to do this even when emotional or physical barriers exist that challenge relationship connectedness.

To develop belonging skills we return to the characteristics of Positive Aging: (a) finding the resources to engage belonging behaviors; (b) making life choices that strengthen interpersonal bonds; (c) employing flexibility to patterns and routines that bring us closer to others even in times of change; and (d) emphasizing the positive to affirm relationship meaningfulness.

Mobilizing Resources for Belonging

Resources for belonging can be enhanced through selectivity, optimization, and compensation (SOC) (see Chapter 2). It is well known that as we age, the number of our social relationships diminishes. This is a form of selectivity; it occurs naturally through processes like the death of family members and friends, as well as when one's living situation becomes more restricted. In the latter case, you may simply lose friends and acquaintances because you are no longer able to interact with them on a regular basis. Or your energy to sustain many friendships and relationships is no longer sufficient; it takes more time and effort to just keep up with your day-to-day routine and the few relationships that are part of that routine.

Recent research in gerontology suggests that it may at times be desirable to consciously disengage from people; a good analogy is a garden: from time to time even your most prized plants need pruning, thinning, and even eliminating so that the healthy plants that remain have room to grow and mature. In fact, researchers in the science of aging suggest that for older adults to maintain healthy psychological functioning into their later years, it is required that they eliminate or "prune" superficial relationships to free up personal resources to devote to relationships that are more meaningful. This phenomenon, known in the scientific literature as socioemotional selectivity theory (Lockenhoff & Carstensen, 2004) is a how Positive Agers find resources to sustain their sense of belonging with advancing age. In other words, you have to let go of some relationships in order to preserve others. The example of Steve and Emma's experience with holiday cards highlights how this works.

PRUNING HOLIDAY CARDS

Prior to retirement, Steve was a social worker who was employed with a local organization that provided services to immigrants. Emma, a nurse, had many friends and acquaintances she had made at the busy medical center where she had been employed for many years. Steve and Emma traveled extensively in Europe and in South America when they were younger. They made many friends from these trips. Each Christmas season they sent traditional holiday cards to all of their family and friends worldwide. Many of these family, friends, associates, community organizations, neighbors, colleagues and coworkers, and international acquaintances reciprocated. Each season these received cards were a source of pride. Steve and Emma would display them prominently in their home on tabletops, hanging from their fireplace, along their walls, and on their kitchen refrigerator. Steve even saved them from year to year and they occupied several boxes that were stored in their garage. Even after they retired and their children had become adults, Steve and Emma kept sending cards to everyone on their extensive list, and this required several weeks' worth of work and many dollars in postage and card purchases. And as their list continued to grow, even though they were no longer traveling, the biggest challenge was keeping track of all of the names and addresses. Steve was not well organized and he had handwritten notes of names scattered around the house, requiring a yearly effort to organize them and update information when people moved or died. In their seventh decade Emma expressed to Steve that she was tired of the holiday card tradition. She cringed when the Christmas season approached because the workload had become so large. She suggested that they cap the number of cards that they sent each year. This bothered Steve terribly because he didn't want to leave anyone out. "What would Randy and Susan think if they didn't get a card from us?" he asked. Emma responded, "We have not seen or interacted with Randy and Steve in over 5 years and they probably just throw our Christmas card away."

After much discussion they came up with a plan. They would cut their holiday card list in half, only sending cards to those people who they interacted with on a regular basis. This eliminated most of their international friends. Steve thought this was okay since these required the greatest postage. Emma also suggested not sending cards to anyone who had not returned a card to them. This eliminated more cards. Soon their list, though still large, was more manageable. Emma also suggested that Steve throw the boxes of cards away since they rarely even looked at these, and when they did, it was only to get addresses. Steve reluctantly did this, but he wanted to save 20 of his favorite cards.

Emma thought this was acceptable. They were both surprised at how this affected their holiday season. It was no longer associated with the burden and anxiety of preparing so many cards.

In this example, Steve and Emma had developed a pattern of sending cards. It had served their needs for a time, but as they grew older and the list grew longer and burdensome, they engaged in selectivity and limited their card sending to only "the most important people." This affirmative life choice freed them up to focus their card-writing process and to limit the amount of energy they spent. Although it was difficult to alter their routine, they experienced a sense of relief as well as enhanced pleasure that allowed them to find more enjoyment during the holiday season. They employed the Positive Aging skill of selectivity to free up resources for living and in doing so enhanced their sense of well-being.

Being more selective about relationships does not mean that you care less about people. It just means that when you no longer have the resources to sustain a large social network, you must make choices to preserve your own quality of life as it relates to belonging by focusing on the most important people in your life.

Being more selective may also help you discover new sources of meaning in close relationships that were not there before. In other words, by focusing on fewer people in your social network, you have added emotional resources to devote to those people. This kind of focusing opens the door to optimization, where your goal is to practice deepening your relationships with people who are the most meaningful to you. The following example of Sam and his decision to change the nature of his relationship with his grandchildren highlights optimization as a Positive Aging principle embedded in SOC.

SAM AND HIS GRANDCHILDREN

Sam, who was a professional accounts manager, worked into his mid-60s. While employed, he did not pay much attention to his grandchildren because he felt he was too busy to devote time to get to know them. His interactions were, at best, confined to holidays and special events that involved them. His children, following Sam's lead, kept the grandkids separate from him as much as possible especially the young infants who seemed to distract him when they visited. Over time, Sam's grandchildren lost interest in him. Father's day, birthdays, and other holidays went by without acknowledgment from either side. When Sam finally did retire, he began to feel the desire to connect with his grandkids. He encouraged his children and grandchildren to visit. At first, this was difficult, because he was almost a stranger to this very young generation. They had developed their own lives and routines and Sam was not part of these. Sam decided that he would try to visit his grandkids in their homes, and that he would pick projects around his children's homes that he could get involved in, to help improve their homes and their living situations. He involved his grandchildren in these projects. Whether it was raking leaves or running errands, Sam encouraged his grandkids to join him. Soon, Sam began to reconnect with his family and he realized how much he valued his grand-children.

Sam's shift of his social and emotional resources to his family occurred as he let go of work and of the social responsibilities that were part of his job. In doing so, he activated *selectivity*, the resource reallocation skill embedded in Positive Aging, in favor of his family relationships. In doing so, he discovered his grandchildren. He then spent time with them and devoted energy to building relationships by applying the interacting-concern-caring behaviors to his grandkids. This represents a form of *optimization*, and through this effort Sam found a hidden treasure of reciprocal support from family and especially from his grandchildren, who got involved with Sam doing projects around their homes.

Making Life Choices That Strengthen Relationships

How we live our lives and where we choose to live affects, to a great degree, our social relationships and ultimately our sense of belonging. Some life decisions may have large consequences; for example, the decision to live in a rural area rather than an urban area will affect your ability to have contact with others and for others to access you. Your sense of belonging is also influenced by your approach to others. For example, you may be a joiner. Becoming a member of your local senior center, taking part in neighborhood activities, or involving yourself in your community will impact how you feel about belonging. Helping others is another approach to the world that is certain to enhance your sense of belonging. In the previous example, Sam's decision to help his children and to involve the grandchildren in this helping process is one example of how doing for others builds connections and fosters belonging.

Positive Agers are aware of how they approach others and the role they play in shaping the kinds of social networks that work for them. In fact, adjusting your lifestyle from time to time makes good sense. This may involve working with your partner (or reflecting on your own if you are partnerless) to review your past lifestyle patterns. In Sam's case above, his life choices previous to retirement focused on work. This became inconsistent when he decided to retire. In reviewing his life his desire to rekindle family relationships became a priority. One might ask the question, why did Sam not nurture his relationships with his children while he was engaged in his career? This question is difficult to answer; however, what is clear is that Sam decided to shift his time resources at a critical juncture following his retirement in favor of his family. Fortunately for Sam, his children supported his lifestyle change.

How you spend your time is a life choice that impacts almost everyone, rich or poor. Are you a person who prefers to invest time in passive activities such as reading, watching television, or working jigsaw puzzles? Or do you prefer more active pursuits that involve others, such as attending classes, going to a social club, going out to eat, attending a class at your senior center, or dancing? These are the kinds of behaviors that are manifestations of who you are, what you are like, and how you prefer doing things with others.

Flexibility in Relationships

Relationships are like your garden. When you go outside and look over your garden, you assess how well it is growing. Are all of your plants getting watered appropriately? Are there weeds proliferating? Do you notice telltale signs of pests? There might be a vegetable or flower emerging. It is exciting to see the first tomato turn red or the beginnings of a squash or zucchini. Relationships are like this, too. We are regularly engaged in assessing and nurturing our relationships, particularly our more meaningful ones. If you telephone a son or a daughter, for example, you may be able to tell in a short space of time if he or she is fine, if this is a good time to talk, or if there is something you might do for him or her. You cultivate relationships by interacting and showing concern and caring. Sometimes a relationship is so strong and healthy that it needs little nurturing, but no matter how strong it is, it will not survive unless you intermittently assess it and determine what you can do to nurture it and keep it strong. Relationships also change, and what might have strengthened a relationship at one point in time may not be as important later in life. Marriages can be like this. What nurtures new marriages may not be the same as nurturing behaviors in marriages that are long-term. We need to assess all of our relationships to know how they need to be cultivated and we need to be flexible when relationships change.

Sometimes relationships take unexpected twists and turns; these are discontinuities that call for your ability to be flexible in your thinking and in your behavior. It is not always possible to detect a problem or see an opportunity for enhancement. All too often, people take close relationships for granted. The following example highlights how flexibility can be helpful in a relationship that needs repair.

DAD NEEDS HELP

Bill is 83 years old and a widower. He has three adult sons, all of whom have benefited from Bill's generosity over the years. Bill is a New Englander and has been a stalwart advocate of the "pull yourself up by your bootstraps" philosophy. He seldom asks for help, nor has he been willing to accept it when it has been offered. His sons recognize this about Bill and they know that their father expects this of them as well. When Bill has extended help to his sons and their families, it is only because Bill has decided that he will help, not because his family has requested help. For example, if Bill notices that his son's yard needs mowing, then he inquires about the lawn mower. If it is broken, he might pay to get it fixed or simply buy a new one. His sons know better than to ask their father for help, but they know that it is important to thank him when he provides help. Bill's youngest son brought this to Bill's attention one day and this led to a heated argument, followed by a long-standing estrangement. Bill refused to speak to or see his youngest son for several years after the argument, even though the son lives less than a mile from Bill. Recently, Bill suffered a stroke that left him partially paralyzed. Bill's two other sons, who live some distance from Bill, were perplexed as to what to do. They spoke to the younger son, but he indicated that he wanted nothing to do with his father. "It would be better off if Dad just died, because he is always going to be the same at receiving help as he is at giving it out—his terms only." Bill's two older sons decided to approach their father and suggest that he call the younger son and "mend his fences." Bill needed his younger son now more than ever. After more encouragement from his two sons, Bill decided to call his third son. Bill asked his son to help him. The son agreed and together they decided that it would be on terms shared by Bill and his son. Bill accepted this and they mended their relationship. Over time Bill's third son became Bill's closest connection in the family.

The example above highlights how the nature of relationships can change over time based on our choices about how we approach one another. In Bill's case, his inflexibility around giving and receiving help became a barrier between him and his youngest son. It took a personal crisis to create an opportunity to act more flexibly. To Bill's credit, he decided that his stubbornness was working against his relationship with his son, so giving his son an opportunity to help him on shared terms was a pivotal act that signaled that Bill did have the capacity to be flexible. This opened the door for their relationship to improve. Your family of origin, your parents and siblings—for better or worse—will always hold a place in your social network. There are many reasons and causes that can estrange you from your family of origin, such as losing contact through geographical separation. As you age, perhaps these family members might be worth rediscovering, provided they are willing to engage in belonging behaviors. More often than not, it is difficult to completely sever these relationships, so finding ways to flexibly construe them can help you optimally age. Finally, in very old age it may simply become impossible to attend to all of the meaningful relationships in your life because your physical or emotional state won't allow it. For example, if you are living in an assisted care community and do not have access to personal transportation, you might be limited in whom you visit or how often. In this case, you may need to involve some *compensatory* strategies which are part of SOC, including talking on the telephone, using the Internet, or sending letters. Through compensation it is possible to engage in the triad of belonging behaviors and sustain relationships, even though you may not be physically present. This represents a creative way to offset your age-related deficits that allows you to continue to deepen important relationships.

In some instances, a compensatory response may be to let go of your responsibility to maintain relationships and allow that to rest with others. Encouraging others to visit with you by making them feel welcome when they do can foster a sense of belonging, even though you may not be able to reciprocate. You can, when visited, show caring and concern and, most of all, gratefulness for the visit. You then become an instrument that nurtures belonging.

Affirming What Is Positive in Relationships

What does it mean to be a friend? A basic building block of friendship is a positive affirming attitude. Almost everyone wants to be with others who help them feel good about themselves and their place in the world. Books have been written on the power of a positive attitude in relationships. One such well-known book is Dale Carnegie's *How to Win Friends and Influence People*. This book is timeless because it centers on strategies designed to make yourself desirable to others by encouraging others to feel good about themselves. They become more interested in you as a consequence. The essential skill here is "interest in others." Carnegie (1950) wrote:

> There is one all-important law of human conduct . . . [that] if obeyed, will bring us . . . constant happiness. . . . The law is this: Always make the other person feel important. . . . Professor William James says: "The deepest principle in human nature is the craving to be appreciated." (p. 93)

Carnegie suggests that we show interest in others by being good listeners. This involves considering the value of the other person as well as affirming why this person is meaningful to you. In families and among close relationships, this affirmation is usually a reaffirmation. My wife's comment to me that "You can never say you love me too many times," applies here. Consistent positive affirmation is the secret to strong relationship bonds and is at the basis of meeting your need to belong.

SHERRILL AND HER MANY FRIENDS

The secretary in my academic office, who is 68 years old, has a picture on her desk of her standing alongside nine same-aged women, on vacation at Disneyland. When I inquired about this picture, I discovered a wonderful example of belonging through lifelong friendships. She explained to me that this group of women, self-named the "US-10," were lifelong friends who still regularly socialized. The pictures here are of the US-10 in high school, and then 40 years later.

These relationships began in childhood and preceded may of the traditional social lifespan events that occur as one matures, such as marriage and childrearing. These friendships started in a tight-knit rural community in Utah. One of the parents of these young girls had a vacant dry cleaning building that was donated as a clubhouse, where they met and nurtured these early friendships. From childhood onward they frequently *interacted*, showing *concern* and *caring* for one another other. For more than six decades they have maintained their friendships, meeting once a month to share stories and socialize, even though they now live in various places across the country.

This powerful "friendship convoy" retains common memories from childhood, high school, marriages, and the birth and raising of children, and now grandchildren and great grandchildren. Individually,

The US-10, 1956.

The US-10, 2001.

they have all faced difficulties. Some of the friends have experienced divorce; others have lost loved ones to death. Financial setbacks have plagued several, as have illnesses and other personal disappointments. However, when a need arises for one, all of the others are there to help. At the same time, these friends are careful not to disrupt established social relationships. The friends are committed to helping each individual strengthen her marriage, build bonds with her children, and stay connected to their church and community. They have managed an artful balance that has sustained their individual well-being and the cohesiveness of the group into their later years. An interesting aspect of this relationship is the traditions the group has established among themselves including shopping, traveling, and celebrating holidays together. They schedule frequent "reunions" where they dress as a unit, wearing matching outfits. They have learned the value of belonging.

This example of life-long friendship is not easy to create or engender, but it shows how substantial the interaction-concern-caring triad can be if practiced as a Positive Aging strategy for friendship building. In the spirit of this example:

- Can you identify a close friendship or set of friendships in your life?

- What are the kinds of things that you do that keep these friendships meaningful?
- How do these friendships address your needs?
- How well do you assist your friend(s) when a need arises?

The challenge in relationships, especially in old age, is that we accumulate experiences with others that are both negative and positive and, sometimes, and with some people, the balance of shared experiences weighs toward the negative. There are reasons for this. First, negative aspects of relationships are initially enticing to talk about and listen to. The reasons for this are varied, including negative talk as a strategy to feel better about yourself when you know that someone is worse off than you, especially when their sad state is partly of their own doing. When something bad happens to another person, this could be construed as evidence that you could be in worse shape than you are right now. Negative issues are sometimes shrouded in secrecy and learning about a secret can be exciting and interesting. Finally, we practice and rehearse our relational style with others. Continued negativity can color all of your conversations and interactions and cause your social network to move away from you. It won't be long before you are alone, even though others may be around you. You are no longer worth paying attention to. Once you are in this state, it is difficult to recover.

Whether maintaining a positive attitude or an affirmative approach to others, or avoiding negativity in relationships, discipline is required. It is essential that you check your thoughts about yourself and others. To gauge where you stand with respect to the valence of your interactions, you can identify some of these by contemplating the following question: How might people who are in the inner circle of your social convoy describe you? If the description is predominantly negative, then this is an area where you could exercise flexibility and begin changing the way you interact with others.

Old age can create constraints on your context. You may be homebound. Your memory could be declining, so making conversations where you are affirming positive aspects of another may be more challenging. You may have recently experienced the loss of a lifelong partner, finding it difficult to take comfort even in existing relationships. It is under such circumstances that Positive Aging strategies can help you affirm the value in relationships.

- Notice pleasant things about people with whom you are interacting and verbalize them.
- Share common positive memories with others.
- Smile. This is a nonverbal sign that you feel positive about the other people.
- Listen. Sometimes simply listening can fill a need to belong in another person and can strengthen relationship bonds.

III. POSITIVE AGING FOR DEALING WITH LOSS AND LONELINESS

Loneliness is an emotion that you experience when you perceive that you are disconnected from or do not belong to your social network or social convoy. An often-used definition of loneliness is that it is a form of emotional dissonance that results from a discrepancy between what you want from your support network and how you perceive that your social support network is functioning. So, in a sense, loneliness is, for most people, a kind of self-focused negativity. Although loneliness can be a chronic emotional condition experienced at any age, it often appears in later life following a discontinuity in your support network, for example, the loss of a spouse to death, a late-life divorce, the death of a sibling, or even the unanticipated death of an adult child. The following example illustrates how loneliness might emerge.

JUDY'S UNANTICIPATED LONELINESS

Judy is a 72-year-old Midwestern housewife. She had been married for 50 years and has three children from the marriage. Several years previously, Judy's husband left Judy for a 34-year-old employee at his office. He announced to Judy that he wanted to split up immediately, and a lengthy divorce process began. Eventually, they were divorced and Judy, who had few resources, lost her home in the settlement and was forced to move to an apartment in the city. Judy felt alone and discouraged, and she believed that her family was lost. She was in a deep depression for almost a year. Toward the end of that year her lack of sleep, poor appetite, and reclusive behavior began to seriously affect her health. At the insistence of one of her adult children who lived in the same city, Judy started seeing a counselor at a local community mental health facility to treat her depression. One of the issues that she and her counselor began working on was helping Judy deal with her profound sense of loneliness.

Judy's loneliness was due to a discontinuity that disrupted her belonging equilibrium. As a result, her sense of meaning was gone. She felt like she belonged to no one, even though she had support from her adult children and several of her siblings. Because Judy regarded the divorce and its aftermath as beyond her perceived sense of control, Judy was left feeling powerless and hopeless. One of her central questions was, "Is my husband leaving me my fault?"

In this case, Judy needed to find a way to make sense of her situation and to mobilize her emotional resources so as to preserve enough capacity to get beyond the divorce, which was now several years past, and rediscover her worth in the present. While it is true that the divorce created objective social isolation, and that this was a serious problem because it reinforced Judy's sense of herself as a flawed person, the counselor encouraged Judy to think of others in her social convoy, namely, her children and siblings, and create ways for them to help her. Judy just needed to find someone in her inner social convoy circle that could assist her in recapturing her lost sense of belonging. As Judy met with her counselor, one such person who was frequently mentioned in their discussion was Judy's brother. He had seemed willing to listen to her in the past when she had been feeling uncomfortable in her marriage and he had offered her a sympathetic ear and positive affirmation as well as some financial support during the divorce process.

Most of Judy's contact with her brother was by phone. He lived in a different state, but powerful social bonds don't restrict social support to only persons who are physically present. Phone calls, as a compensatory process, can be significant in maintaining one's social convoy.

As Judy began to interact more often with her brother and her adult children, they encouraged Judy to talk with neighbors and others who lived in the city. Judy became acquainted with a female near her own age in her apartment complex, who helped her establish some contacts with other neighbors She started feeling more secure as these connections developed, but she feared that she would never be married again given her advanced age and her health problems. Judy's counselor suggested that she try and set that fear aside and replace it with building connections with existing family members and her community. Judy's loneliness and fears about not remarrying slowly diminished as she reconnected with family and built a new support network.

Judy continued to feel a deep loss in her family structure, but she slowly began to move from self-blame to placing blame on her husband, and finally letting blame go altogether. Her efforts to reinitiate her social convoy in a positive way provided her with new insights about her worth as an individual by actualizing Positive Aging characteristics such as mobilizing resources and exercising flexibility.

IV. POSITIVE AGING FOR GRIEF AND BEREAVEMENT

We may be afraid of our own death. Our worst fears may arise, however, when we contemplate the loss of a significant family member or loved one. When a lifelong partner or a spouse dies, the surviving partner will almost always experience a profound sense of loss that has been labeled as grief. Grieving is a deeply personal and emotional process that follows loss. A grieving person is acutely aware of the power of belonging that is embedded in loss. From the perspective of continuity theory described in Chapter 2, grief is a substantial discontinuity in one's innermost world. It is difficult to personally reconcile this kind of loss. The process of grieving is known as bereavement. During bereavement a person mourns or engages in a specific set of behaviors to deal with the loss. Many of these are culture-specific, such as wearing black clothing when we attend funerals. Not all mourning rituals, however, are depressing and negative and some can actually take on a celebration-like feel. For example, the Mexican-American custom of Dia de los Muertos (the Day of the Dead) uses both festiveness and sadness to help reconcile feelings of loss when a loved one dies. An excerpt from John West's book *Mexican-American Folklore* (1988) summarizes this custom:

DIA DE LOS MUERTOS

Families with Mexican roots [take] with them rakes and hoes and water buckets, along with picnic lunches [to the family grave sites]. Prominent also are mounds of flowers in every color imaginable. . . . Graves have their weeds cut; mounds are re-molded and sprinkled with water. Names on wooden crosses . . . are straightened up. . . . Then the family, seated around the grave, has a picnic meal . . . for it is truly a family gathering, a [symbolic] visit with members of the family who have "gone ahead." (p. 52)

The loss of a loved one can occur at any time during your life; however, it is more likely when you are old. This is where issues of aging affect not only the nature of belonging but how your need to belong is impacted by a discontinuity like the death of a loved one. Positive Aging considers death as a natural part of life and surviving and thriving following the loss of a loved one requires skills that involve mobilizing resources, making affirmative life choices, employing flexibility, and emphasizing the positives.

Researchers studying grief and bereavement have identified several key strategies that people use to get through this process (Carr, Nesse, & Wortman, 2005). In Changing Lives of Older Couples (CLOC) (Bonnano et al., 2002; Carr, Nesse, & Wortman, 2005; Boerner, Wortman, & Bonnano, 2005), a study that considered a group of 185 older persons in the Detroit-Chicago area who had recently lost a spouse to death, those who fared the best through such a loss were "resilient" grievers engaged in Positive Aging behaviors. By using their skills, many of these individuals had rediscovered meaning in their lives in as little as three months after the loss. Here is the bereavement process they used, as adapted from research reports from the CLOC study. (a) They *mobilized their personal resources* by tempering their emotional reaction to the loss through reframing it as a natural part of the life course and by focusing on memories of their loved one which could give them strength to continue on with their journey in life. Many used their religious beliefs to give them comfort. (b) *They made affirmative life choices* to stay engaged in the world. This involved getting support and meaning from family, friends, and others in their world whom they could rely on for emotional support and to help them transition from being coupled to being single. They discovered new activities to engage in while single and they shaped activities that they traditionally did with their spouse in such a way that they could still find meaning in them, even though the spouse was no longer present. (c) They acted *flexibly* about the loss, using strategies such as humor by recalling memories that made them laugh or think fondly of their lost partner (Ong, Bergeman, & Bisconti, 2004). They altered their living contexts to make it easier to live alone by making changes such as downsizing their space needs, and eliminating unneeded objects (e.g., the second car). (d) They focused on the *positives* when they spoke to others and emphasized their new life following the loss. This was done not by denying that the loss occurred; in fact, several people cherished keepsakes from their departed loved one that reminded them what the departed spouse had given to them, including the hope that they might find happiness following this loss. These "resilient" grievers were able to find meaning in and cope with one of the most challenging developmental stages of the life span. Learning to deal with loss was, for many, an ultimate lesson in the cultivation of a sense of belonging, even in the presence of permanent loss, through principles of Positive Aging.

Chapter 5

STRATEGY #5: BY GIVING AND RECEIVING HELP, YOU PROMOTE GROWTH

I. HELPING

Helping is part of the fabric of everyday living and it is one of the ways that we strengthen bonds between family and friends, our neighbors, those in our community, and even people we do not know but whom we help through charitable organizations. Helping also extends to animals, plants, our environment, and our world. We also help ourselves. Evidence for this is in the "self-help" movement. As you read this book, you are helping yourself feel happier and healthier.

Another label for helping that is found in the philosophical and scientific literature is *altruism*, which connotes an orientation of concern and caring toward others. In religion altruism is a universal virtue. Eastern religious philosophy places altruism at the center of its spiritual traditions. In Buddhism (Soka-Gakkai, 2007) altruism occurs when you consider your own suffering and then use this knowledge to cultivate empathy for others.

> Buddhism views altruism as an expression of one's awakening to one's true self and . . . that it stems from compassion, appreciation and a sense of interconnection. (p. 1)

A behavioral manifestation of altruism (or helping) in the United States is volunteering. Volunteerism has its roots in the foundation of our country, with long-standing organizations devoted to volunteer activities such as the Salvation Army and the Volunteers of America (Ellis, 1990). The Volunteers of America program was founded in 1896 by the pioneering social reformers Ballington and Maud Booth. Volunteers of America has become one of the largest service providers in the United States today. It actively operates programs that address pressing social needs in our contemporary world by helping abused and neglected children, assisting homeless individuals and families, and serving the elderly, youth at risk, and people with developmental and physical disabilities. It is estimated that between 2 and 3 million people across the United States receive services from the Volunteers of America.

Policy makers who investigate the public health impact of volunteers have found that our country depends heavily on their support. The Department of Labor reported that in 2006 more than 60 million adults in the United States reported engaging in volunteer activities (U.S. Bureau of Labor Statistics, 2006). Volunteerism is an important social resource and is a $6 billion industry in the United States and growing annually (Corporation for National and Community Service, 2007). Whether rich or poor, healthy or sick, young or old, virtually all of us have been touched by volunteerism, either as a recipient or as a provider.

In addition to the benefits that those in need receive from volunteers, it is clear that volunteering is associated with emotional, intellectual, and spiritual benefits for the volunteers themselves. With respect to knowledge, Hindu traditions teach that engaging in volunteerism can be a source of insight about oneself and others:

> Since God resides in each person, service of humanity [is] a form of worship. Voluntary sewa (or service), as a personal undertaking, is thus enjoined on every Sikh man, woman and child. It has become an ethical commitment, for followers of this faith, without expectation of monetary rewards, or as a shortcut to spiritual salvation. Altruism is seen as the "essence of all knowledge." [Singh, 2007]

From the science of psychology, study after study has documented that volunteering is associated with positive late-life adjustment and is a resource for finding greater meaning and purpose in life (Morrow-Howell, Hinterlong, Rozario, & Tang, 2003). In one study conducted by Dulin, Hill, Andersen, and Rasmassen (2001) over 100 low-income older adults who were participants in the Americorp National Senior Companion and Foster Grandparent programs were surveyed. As a volunteer services arm of Salt Lake County (Utah) Aging Services, Senior Companions provide help to the frail elderly in a variety of contexts including household chores, financial management, and caregiver respite. In the Foster Grandparent program, older volunteers provide assistance to at-risk children and teens. To be eligible to join both of these programs, applicants must be 65 years or older and must document that their income is below the poverty line.

The 100 older Senior Companion/Foster Grandparent volunteers were, by self-report, financially poor and not physically well. Nearly one third of the volunteers were first-generation immigrants who spoke little English. On the Life Satisfaction in the Elderly Scale (LSES), a standardized and nationally normed measure of well-being across six areas of functioning including meaning, social contacts, mood, self-concept, health, and finances, Senior Companion/Foster Grandparent volunteers scored below the national norm on health and finances; however, when queried about meaning, social contacts, mood, and self-concept their scores were substantially above LSES national norms. Like the study of Dulin, Hill, Andersen, and Rasmassen (2001), other investigations into the effects of helping behavior have found evidence that regular volunteering can make you:

- happier;
- healthier;
- easier to live with;
- better at taking care of yourself and others.

One intriguing study even found that volunteers live longer than nonvolunteers. Harris and Thoresen (2005) examined data from the Longitudinal Study of Aging (LSOA), composed of over 7,000 adults 70 years and older. These researchers contrasted longevity trends in those older persons who engaged in volunteering in contrast to a matched comparison group who were never volunteers. Volunteers in this study were at lower risk for dying prematurely than were the nonvolunteers. The researchers reasoned that volunteers develop a sense of belonging or connectedness that promotes longevity. They also found that volunteers perceived themselves as more engaged with life than nonvolunteers. This study suggests that volunteering is associated with a stronger sense of meaning and purpose in life which translates into enhanced longevity.

The motivation to volunteer naturally emerges from maturational processes. Two ideas are important here. First, you will be motivated to help others to the degree that you are able to put, at least temporarily, the needs of someone else above your own personal needs. Erikson, Erikson, and Kivnick (1986) proposed eight stages of development. One of the eight stages, the desire to be altruistic or to help others, gets stronger as you grow older and you are mature enough to begin to think about the world from a perspective that is not focused only on yourself. Erikson labeled this stage "Generativity versus Self-Absorption." You may at this time of your life be the one who takes on the responsibility and the task of transmitting values to others in the younger generation that will help them to get along in life. Generativity is being concerned enough about the welfare of others that you take the time to teach those younger than you how to glean from the past important ideas and principles that have worked to preserve your well-being. This includes altruism.

The second idea comes from the final stage of the theory of Erikson, Erikson, and Kivnick (1986), "Integrity versus Despair." In the twilight of life you may begin thinking about who you are, where you have been in life, and how you want to be remembered by others. If you live into very old age, you may also need assistance maintaining your home or performing self-care tasks. Due to your age-related deficits you could be an instrument through which others, younger and more physically able than yourself, can lend you a helping hand. This component of helping—the ability to receive help from others—may seem paradoxical. How can receiving help be altruistic? The answer to this question is easily understood: If you want to help others mature, there will come a time when you can encourage them to engage in helping you to negotiate life's tasks and challenges so that they can learn what it means to be altruistic.

Interestingly, most of us are taught that we should be self-sufficient, and "pull ourselves up by our own bootstraps" when things are difficult. This second idea, however, is just the opposite. It involves a profoundly important concept, that is, letting people help you is a form of altruism. In fact, some theorists have surmised that developing the skill to receive help is as important as the act of giving help itself (Shinn & Toohey, 2003).

II. POSITIVE AGING AND HELPING

Helping not only aids others, but it is good for you as well. Positive Agers know how both to give and to receive help. The next step is to understand how Positive Aging characteristics can assist you in becoming an effective helper. This involves (a) discovering ways in which you are uniquely suited to help; (b) learning what it means to receive help and why being a good "help receiver" is just as important as giving help; and (c) knowing how to manage the dynamic of help giving and help receiving.

The Ways You Are Suited for Helping

What are the characteristics of a helper? We can specify these by examining a famous help-giver, Florence Nightingale, a nurse who began her career in 1851 and viewed nursing as a divine calling. She cared for poor and indigent people and advocated for improved medical care in infirmaries in England and for reform of the Poor Laws. The legacy of Florence Nightingale illustrates the characteristics of altruism: (a) a desire to help others; (b) putting the needs of others before our own needs; (c) acting on our desires to help; and (d) engaging our resources in the helping process.

The Skill of Help Giving

At its most basic level, helping requires finding a reason and a place to provide aid. I've used the term *altruism* to describe motivations to help. Altruism can be cultivated by reflecting on your life and identifying those who have helped you in the past. "Why did that person help me?" "How did I benefit from receiving help?" Such introspection may stimulate your desire to help someone else in need. People commonly get involved in helping through encouragement from others. Over two thirds of people who volunteer in the United States do so through organizations such as the Red Cross or the American Cancer Society (U.S. Bureau of Labor, 2007). A solicitation might also come from a more personal source: a neighbor, a friend, or a family member. The next part of helping is to identify a place or a person to help. This is usually where an unmet need exists. Once identified, you can start helping. But is helping that simple? What if you are reluctant to be a helper?

If you are feeling reluctant about helping, you may want to examine barriers behind this reluctance. A few of the reasons that people report that make them reluctant to give help are:

- I don't have the time to devote to helping other people.
- I'm too sick to help other people.
- I don't know anyone who needs help.
- I'm afraid to help others people because I'm not sure how they will take it.
- I've never received help in my life, so why should I help others?
- I've had experiences where my efforts to help were rebuffed.
- I have too many troubles in my life to devote time to helping others.
- If I'm always helping others I won't get my own needs met.

A commonality in these barriers is the fear of lack of resources to help, lifestyle patterns that do not include helping, rigid thinking about what might be negative consequences from helping, and a negative attitude about being a helper. Positive Aging characteristics can be directly applied to overcome these barriers and pave the way for you to infuse acts of helping into your lifestyle that will produce positive psychological consequences.

Mobilizing Resources for Helping

The statements above reveal reasons that may prevent you from engaging in helping. Some are, indeed, realities that make help giving more challenging. One is that in old age your emotional and physical capacity may have diminished to the extent that you may not feel you have the energy to help others. It takes resources to engage in helping behaviors. Lack of energy can be magnified when you watch television or listen to the radio and hear about heroic acts that people perform. For example, there are not-for-profit organizations like the Peace Corps that require travel and sometimes working in harsh conditions as part of the volunteer experience. Indeed, sacrifice of oneself and one's resources is a trademark of the Peace Corps. If you are gauging your interests in helping based on this kind of metric, it is easy to conclude that helping is not for you. This may be especially true if you have a chronic health condition, are homebound because of your advanced age, or are on a limited budget. In these instances this scale of helping may simply not be possible.

One way to find resources for helping is to employ selectivity, optimization, and compensation (SOC) from Chapter 1 and find selective ways to volunteer. For example, you might inquire at your local senior center if there are opportunities for helping or volunteering that do not involve travel or expending resources other than your time. The following example of a volunteer activity, found on the Internet, highlights one way that a person who is otherwise confined to home might be engaged in helping.

PHONE-VOLUNTEER EXAMPLE

St. Vincent de Paul Society provides its members with opportunities to participate in multiple volunteer services directed to the poor, with a unique focus on one-to-one personal services through home visitation, aid, referral services, support, and problem-solving. Consider volunteering in Phone Outreach:

PHONE OUTREACH VOLUNTEER
Reach out and touch someone! We need folks who like to chat on the phone and call past and potential donors to our thrift stores. This is an as-needed role. You can either work at our main office or work from the comfort of your own home. This is a great opportunity for volunteers who want to do volunteer work but cannot commit to a set schedule or need to be at home. You must have a pleasant, friendly phone manner, work well independently, and have a willingness to smile and dial.

This activity could be amenable to older persons who have disabilities. For example, if you have hearing or vision impairment, you could use a telephone that amplifies hearing and is designed for vision-impaired dialing. Also, you could create a script that would make engaging in a dialogue easier.

Making a Life Choice to Be a Helper

If you have a life history of volunteering, then it is likely you will volunteer in old age. Erikson, Erikson, and Kivnick (1986) found this to be the case in participants from the Berkeley Guidance Study.

> Several women who once volunteered in such organizations as the Red Cross and the Community Chest now channel their energies into assisting the needy elderly by delivering "meals on wheels," visiting in nursing homes, and knitting for residents of convalescent homes. One woman in her late seventies says, "I am still able to drive, so why shouldn't I deliver these things? You get in contact with people who kind of get you down, but some of them—they just want to talk . . . society really should involve all these old people in things [more often]. Get their minds off their worries" . . . this demonstration of old-age initiative is closely tied to the expression of "grand-generativity" . . . they are not simply maintaining lifelong involvements. They are doing so in a fashion that shows sincere and effective concern for others. (p. 178)

If you want to become a volunteer, consider strategies for working such a commitment into your lifestyle. Lifestyle behaviors involve persistent patterns of acting and behaving that continue over time, and that fit your other lifestyle interests and values. A beginning point is to identify your values.

List five things that you have valued over your lifetime (three examples have been provided)

- Example: My education
- Example: My family
- Example: My religious beliefs
- _____
- _____
- _____

- _____
- _____

Identify ways that you can support these values through volunteer efforts or helping. These behaviors might include tutoring at an elementary school (because I value "Education"); making deliveries, phone calls, or other types of assistance through your church (because I value "My religious beliefs"); or even helping a family member in need (because I value "My family"). Make a list of volunteer behaviors that appeal to your values system:

- Example: Reading to others who have difficulty reading
- Example: Baking goods and giving them to elderly shut-ins downtown
- _____
- _____
- _____

By matching your values with your behaviors, it is possible to identify volunteer opportunities that will be enjoyable. Volunteer activities can be found in many places: in contexts where seniors gather (senior citizen centers), churches, government charities, youth organizations, and so forth through higher education (local community colleges or universities in your area). If you are interested in volunteering, then outlets for engaging your interests are there.

Also, to engage a lifestyle behavior, you need to commit to doing it over a prescribed period of time because, more likely than not, your interest in the volunteering will ebb and flow before it becomes a solid part of your lifestyle behavior patterns. This prescribed time period might be anywhere from 1 month to 1 year or longer. At the end of this period, you can reevaluate whether volunteering is something you want to continue or whether you would prefer trying something else. Commitment is the key here, even if you are doing something that you believe in and enjoy doing; you still need to commit yourself to it.

There are long-term rewards associated with volunteering. Those who make volunteering a life-span pursuit are considered to be generous, and generosity is associated with a number of positive outcomes including a rich social support network of those whom you have helped in the past. The science of gerontology has discovered that generous people are, for the most part, positive and highly motivated to do good, and experience well-being in old age (Penner, 2002). Becoming a generous person, however, does not occur without effort or sacrifice, but engaging in volunteer activities is one of the first steps to cultivating generosity within yourself.

Flexibility in Helping

Engaging in helping requires flexibility and, in the same vein, those who volunteer develop greater flexibility. Flexibility is the capacity to invoke new strategies of behaving and thinking that promote better adaptation. The goal of flexibility is to activate sources of meaning through thinking in different ways. Given that it may be challenging to discover new meaning in old patterns and behaviors, there may be variations in behaviors that you can engineer that can stimulate meaning. The following summary of a study of longevity in nursing home residents who are given the opportunity to care for a plant highlights how helping can produce enhanced quality of life in elders who are stereotypically defined as "needy," "rigid," and relatively unmotivated to enhance their own well-being.

CARING ENHANCES LONGEVITY

Judith Rodin and Ellen Langer (1977) recruited 91 nursing home residents from a single nursing home and divided them into three groups. Members of the first group were given a houseplant and instructed to care for it. Members of the second group received a houseplant, but its care was institutionalized (a nurse watered and tended it). Members of a third group received no plant. Anecdotal reports suggested that residents in the group where they cared for the houseplant became happier and more active than those in the other two groups. After 18 months residents in group 1 who cared for the houseplant showed better health and fewer had died, in contrast to the two comparison groups. The authors suggested that this was due to the perception of increased control of the residents in the houseplant care group. A related explanation could be that the residents in the houseplant care group engaged in an altruistic behavior that then engendered a

100

sense of meaning and purpose. Being responsible for helping a plant to live and grow was a source of meaning for those nursing home residents in the plant care group.

This study is important because it underscores the fact that you are never too old or too impaired to provide aid or help. Judging from the happiness that was generated, asking residents to care for a simple houseplant would strongly argue for the benefits of altruism, even in patients who have substantial disturbance in memory or cognitive functioning. Helping, therefore, is a universal quality that may transcend many of the impairments of old age.

Focusing on the Positives in Helping

Although almost everyone has been a helper at some point, your present situation may be such that you have not had a recent opportunity to help. If you are among the very old, you may be in need of help. If this is the case, but you find that you are interested in improving your daily outlook through helping, you've accomplished the first step, which is to find the desire to help. As you cultivate this desire, a second step is to find internal resources for helping. This will likely mean taking the time that you spent on something else and shifting it to helping. To aid you in working through some of the barriers that may stand in your way of helping, the following steps may be useful: (a) decide on specific ways to help; (b) make contact with volunteer organizations; or (c) work with a service coordinator who can help you identify a way to volunteer that fits your situation and your resources. A service coordinator can assist you in your efforts to engage in volunteerism by:

- Identifying motivational materials about helping or volunteering.
- Connecting you to a volunteer organizational meeting where you can obtain more information about how and where you can volunteer.

As you engage in volunteer experiences that interest you, it won't be long before you create a positive attitude toward your newfound interest in volunteering. Your interest or affirmative attitude about volunteerism will become another resource that will aid you to engage in helping. The scientific literature confirms this. The fact is, even if you start helping begrudgingly—but you do it anyway—you can still reap benefits, as the following example highlights:

DOUG'S EXPERIMENT WITH HELPING

Doug has had a difficult life that has lacked stability. His early up-bringing was in a foster home, where his foster parents cared little about him. He had difficulty in school and never graduated from high school. When he dropped out, he became part of a gang that committed a number of crimes in the city where he lived. He engaged in increased criminal behavior and spent some time in prison. He vowed after that experience never to get caught up in this kind of trouble again, so he started working as an entry-level driver for a parcel delivery company. He stayed with this company for over 20 years until it was sold to a larger corporation, which then laid him off. For the next 10 years he worked varying part-time and full-time jobs as a delivery driver. Doug had been married twice and both marriages ended in divorce. Doug was unhappy and lonely, living in an apartment near where he worked. One day, Doug noticed that he was having trouble with his vision, so he went to an eye doctor who informed him that he had macular degeneration and would be nearly blind in about a year. This news devastated Doug because it meant that he would need to find employment that did not involve driving.

As Doug's disease progressed he became more isolated and dwelled on resentments he had about his foster parents, his early life, and his failed marriages. He had three children from these marriages, but he had not had contact with them for 10 years. Doug was encouraged by his physician to attend a support group at the hospital, where he could get some assistance in "learning to live" with his disease. Doug reluctantly attended this group. The first meeting had a surprising impact on him. He realized that there were many people, some of whom were younger than he, who were struggling with this disease.

One of the programs that Doug became particularly interested in was one in which those individuals who were in more severe stages of the disease were partnered with those whose vision was more functional. Doug was paired with an older woman who was nearly blind. Part of Doug's role was to visit with this woman, Margaret, and help her with household chores and other tasks. In turn, Margaret taught Doug about his disease and ways he could cope.

Doug enjoyed the opportunity to help Margaret and it was not long before they became close friends. As Doug's vision became worse, Margaret was there for encouragement. Doug and Margaret initiated a conversation club in the support group that discussed current events and other topics of interest as a positive way to keep socially and intellectually active even though their vision was declining. Doug began to feel that he was a valued member of this group and although his eyesight got steadily worse, his mood and his outlook on life improved. He enjoyed helping and feeling needed by the group.

This story shows how even a bitter person can become engaged in volunteering, with the effect of producing a positive sense of well-being. The impact of altruistically motivated helping as a way to find peace of mind comes from moving the focus of one's psychological resources from self-concerns to a more outward concern for the welfare of others. Not only is this a powerful self-help strategy, but it is a compelling area where future professional counseling for older adults might move. You can test this idea for yourself. Engage in a helping opportunity that you don't particularly like doing (even for yourself). Notice how this otherwise unrewarding behavior becomes more interesting and fulfilling and induces a positive view about yourself as a helper, as well as in the individual whom you are assisting.

The Skill of Help Receiving

Everyone at every age needs help at some time, although the longer you live the more likely it is that you will need help. Figure 5.1 on the next page indicates over half of the people who are 85 years and older need some form of help.

The acknowledgment of that need is noted in the saying from George Washington Carver: "How far you go in life depends on your being tender with the young, compassionate with the aged, sympathetic with the striving and tolerant of the weak and strong. Because someday in life you will have been all of these."

To think that receiving help is desirable or that it comes easy does not take into account how you might have been taught about the

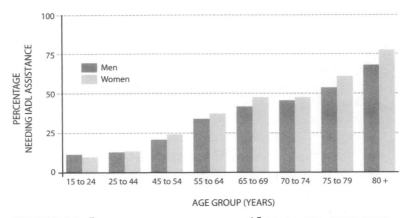

FIGURE 5.1. PERCENTAGE OF PEOPLE AGED 15 YEARS AND OLDER WHO REQUIRE ASSISTANCE WITH ACTIVITIES OF DAILY LIVING (ADL).

nature of helping. The following sayings illustrate barriers to receiving help:

- Never accept help from strangers.
- It's better to give than to receive.
- Pull yourself up by your boot straps.
- Live free or die.

These are social imprints that can limit your views about receiving help. Such statements or social rules may have a purpose in certain contexts, for example, you would never want to help yourself by taking candy out of a baby's hand just to satisfy your own craving for sweets. Such sayings, however, might also set a tone for the following: (1) Don't accept help even when it is offered, and (2) you should always be able to solve your own problems.

For some, a sense of independence and maintaining that independence represent a strong barrier to receiving help. The statement "Live free or die" can be found on car license plates in New Hampshire. It is the official motto of the state, adopted in 1945, and it speaks to the ideal of independence that is part of the American dream and the expectation that we have the right to live and to choose as we see fit. For some, receiving help might be construed as acknowledging the need of support from another person. Such dependency could work against one's inalienable right to live one's own lifestyle. For such a person, receiving help, even if that help is needed, could represent a substantial challenge to freedom and independence.

People vary in their willingness to receive help. The likelihood of asking for help will depend, to a great degree, on how comfortable a person is with receiving help. In the following exercise, you can explore how willing you are to receive help.

WHEN WOULD I CONSIDER RECEIVING HELP? EXERCISE:

Rate these according to the following scale: A (1) indicates that you would never consider receiving help for this, (2) you would rarely consider receiving help, (3) you would consider receiving help from time to time, (4) you would consider receiving help, and (5) you would always consider receiving help.

RECEIVING HELP
- Accept a monetary gift from someone who is poorer than me ____
- Help cleaning my gutters from a friend when my poor vision makes the task dangerous ____
- Help from a stranger when I am struggling to cross the street ____
- Help from a neighbor to buy groceries if I could not afford them ____
- Accept money from a grandchild to pay my bills ____
- Receive blood from a stranger for a transfusion ____
- Accept the donation of a kidney from a stranger for a life saving surgery ____

Not only is it important to learn how to receive help as we age to maintain our functioning, but it is important to provide opportunities for others to learn how to help by becoming an instrument through which help can be given. An analogy from child rearing might facilitate an understanding of this concept. When children are young they are often eager to help. They might want to help their father do the vacuuming or gardening. Their skills may not be such that they can actually aid in the performance of these tasks, but by showing a willingness to help, they are learning important principles of living and are exhibiting a developing maturity. In a learning context, such a willing child might be allowed to help even though the child's efforts are counterproductive with regard to the task. The same can also be the case in old age. Perhaps a younger person asks you if you need help with a task. It may be that you can perform the task, even though it may be difficult. It may be, however, that you discern that this younger person's desire to help is an altruistic gesture that you want to cultivate so you allow them to help.

How to Receive Help Graciously

Positive Agers are both help givers and help receivers. Positive Aging characteristics can be applied to facilitate helping. These characteristics can also be applied to receiving help.

Of the Positive Aging characteristics, flexibility is, perhaps, the most important in optimal help receiving. In this instance flexibility comes from understanding how and why people want to help you and then knowing how to respond or to acknowledge that you are willing to receive such help. To know how to receive help requires that you are able to think and act flexibly.

Like volunteering or providing assistance, receiving help can be initiated with the idea in mind that you are making it possible for someone who is interested in you or cares about you to show caring by helping you. To refuse help when it is offered may send the message that you are still independent, but it could also convey that you don't value the offer of help. Furthermore, when you spurn a sincere offer of help, there is the possibility that you have denied a growth opportunity. This insight can be seen in the following story:

GRANDCHILDREN WANT TO HELP

Dixie is 55 years old and has been married to Jeff for 35 years. Dixie is a social worker and Jeff is a retired schoolteacher. Dixie's mother, Donna, became widowed 1 year ago. Donna is 87 years old and suffers from disabling chronic back pain. For most of her life, Donna has been fiercely independent and even in her old age she is reluctant to receive help from anyone but her daughter. Dixie, who visits her mother daily, has been cleaning Donna's house for nearly a year. Jeff and Dixie talked about how to involve their own children in Donna's care.

They reasoned that Donna's grandchildren could benefit from opportunities to serve. Dixie suggested to her mother that her grandkids would like to help her. After some coaxing, Donna agreed, and Dixie set up a schedule for her children to help Donna with various tasks that ranged from yard work to fixing dinner, to housework. Unbeknownst to Dixie, however, each time her children came to "help" Grandma Donna, she paid them $50 and instructed them, "Don't tell your mother or father about this money." This pattern persisted for several months, until Dixie discovered that her mother had been paying her children and that her children had decided not to tell Dixie about it.

At first, Dixie was furious, but then she thought about it and decided that perhaps her children were not quite mature enough to understand that Grandma did not know how to receive help very well, and this was the only way that Grandma felt comfortable about receiving this help. At an opportune time Dixie spoke with her children and revealed that she was aware that they had been receiving money. Dixie did not scold her children, nor did she want Grandma Donna to stop accepting help. So, Dixie suggested that the kids continue accepting Grandma's payments, but that they put the money into a fund that could be used to buy things that Grandma needed and to keep the house nice with occasional flowers and other decorations that Grandma liked. This strategy worked well, even though Grandma never became aware that her money was being returned to her in this way.

Dixie was flexible in her attitude toward her children, her mother, and the act of helping. Grandma Donna had not been able to step outside of her pattern of always giving back more than she received. The children, however, were teachable and Dixie had suggested a way to help Grandma while at the same time building altruism. Such an approach and attitude can make receiving help as important as giving help in becoming a Positive Ager.

One way to develop a positive attitude about receiving help is to reflect on times that you extended a helping hand to others in need. It is likely you will generate positive memories, pleasant emotions, and even a sense of gratefulness that you were able to help. To indicate that you don't want, need, or deserve an offer of help may work against someone who is trying to become more altruistic and may make you seem ungrateful.

Of course, helping may not directly involve the receiver. Take, for instance, the act of donating blood. When you make the donation it is unlikely that you will ever see the recipient of this source of help. You are giving of yourself freely, without expectation of any reward in return. This is, perhaps, the highest form of altruism. Learning to receive an offer of help and developing an approach to the helper that is affirmative will generate powerful positive emotions that will extend to the helper and to you.

When and How to Give and Receive Help

Why, when, and how are you comfortable giving help? Under what conditions would you allow someone else to help you? Your response to these questions can provide you with insight into both your comfort level around giving help and receiving help, as well as your ability to engage in these Positive Aging behaviors. Helping is an acquired skill. We learn about it when we are young and continue to refine our abilities to give and receive help across our lifetimes. To be a good giver and receiver of help requires cultivating resources including flexibility, sensitivity, and a positive attitude.

This highlights a critical point: Some forms of behaving have the appearance of helping but emanate from a self-serving source. For example, you may be familiar with a person who gives help no matter what the situation or condition. This person has learned that helping is good, but cannot stop from giving help even when it is not needed or wanted. At the same time, there are people who always want help, who are overly dependent and needy, and who get their needs met through the good will of others. These two kinds of actions are not helping behaviors because they involve meeting one's own needs. "Other focused" helping involves; (a) a mature awareness of needs in yourself and in others; (b) understanding that people value their freedom and independence and helping should not constrain these; and (c) knowing that receiving help is a gift and gifts are not an expectation or an earned commodity. Helping involves sensitivity and a focus on others even when you are the help receiver. Below are a few questions about giving and receiving help that you can ask yourself. These come from a Positive Aging framework that can be used to gauge your motivations and your approach to giving and receiving help.

- Does a need exist?
- How much help is needed?
- What are my reasons for helping?
- Why is this person helping me? What are his/her motivations?
- What kind of relationship do I have with the giver or the receiver of help?
- Will my relationship change with this person if I help (or if I accept help)?
- What is affirmative or positive about the help I am giving or receiving?

III. GRANDPARENTING: A GOOD TIME FOR GIVING AND RECEIVING HELP

I've noted that there are skills one can use to become a better help giver and receiver. One of the roles that many of us will experience as we grow old is grandparenting. Grandparents both give and receive help. What follows is an application of the Positive Aging strategy of helping applied to grandparenting.

Grandparents give help. A recent AARP phone survey identified 1,500 respondents who indicated that they were grandparents (AARP, 2002). This survey asked about the kinds of activities and conversations that these grandparents engaged in with their grandkids. Topics of discussion involved school, values, how to stay out of trouble, and deeper issues like spirituality and getting ahead in life. Grandparents reported valuing the act of sharing advice. In fact, 65 percent of the respondents reported that the focus of most of their conversations was on helping their grandkids deal with issues. A minority (20 percent) reported that they also involved their grandchildren in helping them solve their own problems. Perhaps these grandparents also understood that creating opportunities for grandkids to help can be as valuable as the giving of advice when it comes to building positive character traits.

From a Positive Aging perspective, grandparenting is an ideal setting in which not only giving, but receiving help can occur. If you are a grandparent and your grandchildren are young, it is probably quite natural for you to think primarily of giving. Grandparents love giving to their grandchildren. This giving might come in the form of gifts or in time spent with grandchildren or a kind of affirmation that tells the grandchild that he or she is special. Grandparents can also be a vehicle for learning early lessons in altruism. The story of Dixie and Donna in this chapter highlights this idea. Following is the summary of a film from the Utah Sundance Film Festival in 2006 titled *No. 2*, which also illustrates this point.

NO. 2

Nanna Maria is a single grandparent from Fiji. She lives with her granddaughter in a home in New Zealand. Nanna dreams of her youth in the islands of Fiji. She remembers the past because she is troubled about the present. Her front door is sealed in Fijian tradition after the death of her husband and her own children have lost the traditions of Fiji in their lives. They also have strong animosity toward one another and do not regularly visit Nanna. To remedy this situation, Nanna comes up with an idea. She will ask her grandchildren (cousins who range in age from 16 to 23) to throw a party for her in traditional Fijian fashion with the roasting of a pig, music, and celebration. The grandchildren are reluctant because they are not familiar with these traditions, but Nanna teaches them the basics and they decide to throw the party for her. There are lots of challenges including the requirement that the grandchildren bring their parents together to attend. The movie culminates as the traditional festivities begin. The grandchildren make many mistakes, such as tearing down the ceremonially sealed door to make it easier to enter the house and performing ancient Fijian dancing to modern music. Many hidden benefits ensue as the grandkids push their parents to interact with each other even though some of them have vowed never to talk with their siblings again.

The party helps the grandchildren rediscover their parents (who also mend fences with their own siblings), learn the traditions of Fiji and find ways to give back to those who have given to them in the past. In a final act, Nanna bestows a family heirloom upon a grandchild that passes on her legacy and the legacy of her culture to this emerging generation. Within a few days after the party Nanna dies in her sleep. She has achieved her final objective through the help that was given by her grandchildren.

In *No. 2* director Toa Fraser cleverly captures a variation on the grandparent theme, that is, how to facilitate growth in others through the process of receiving help. In this film Nanna knows that she can use her grandparental influence to persuade her grandchildren to help her. She graciously seeks and receives this assistance with the knowledge that in helping her, the grandchildren have an opportunity to learn important life lessons and mature in the process.

Chapter 6

STRATEGY #6: YOU CAN
FORGIVE YOURSELF
AND OTHERS

I. FORGIVENESS

Forgiveness has been associated with spiritual and emotional healing since the dawn of mankind. As a life tenet, it has been deemed by religious scholars and practitioners as essential to spirituality and a prerequisite to salvation. Christianity is built on the principles of forgiveness. The Bible summarizes it as a specialized form of empathy:

> Be kind and compassionate to one another, forgiving each other (Ephesians 4:32)

Kindness, compassion, mercy, sympathy, and equanimity are all expressions of forgiveness. It is difficult to be "kind" if you are not forgiving. If you have a life pattern of forgiveness, others will view you as "kind."

Forgiveness has also been of interest in psychology and neuroscience. Researchers have postulated that there is a set of processes between brain structure and function that allows a person to think and feel in ways that promote forgiveness (Newberg, et al., 2000). In psychotherapy, forgiveness, which has also been described as "letting go," is an intervention used for treating psychological disorders.

As a sociological construct, researchers have argued that forgiveness is the glue that binds people together and ameliorates personal differences (Griswald, 2007). After you err or offend someone—a family member, a lover, a friend, or even an acquaintance—and you want to repair the relationship, you employ forgiveness. The same is true for those who have offended you. Over your lifetime you will forgive others, but you will also need to seek forgiveness if you want to be happy. In the absence of forgiveness it would be difficult, if not impossible, for people to live together in harmony. This is particularly true in our modern capitalist society where competition and self-interest are ideals that are emphasized. In competition, the goal is to be the first or the best or to win over others. If you are a successful competitor you distinguish yourself from the group. Some people do this by taking advantage of others, but even in the fairest of competitions there is always a winner and a loser. The winner receives the prize and the loser often fades away unrecognized. Competition, of course, is not all bad; it drives us to do better and, for some, to accomplish great things. But it does so by putting our abilities up against others', with the metric of success being the accumulation of winnings that support one's self-interests. The competitive spirit does not tolerate being outdone by others, nor does it tolerate one's own personal failures or the inability to reach an individual goal or objective. There is no mercy in competition. If you fail or fall short, you lose.

Forgiveness is, in many ways, counter to the competitive mentality. It involves considering the needs of others and even reconciling with others. Forgiveness promotes the needs of the group over the needs of the individual. It is inclusive in so far as forgiveness brings people together on the same level through the strengthening of positive emotional bonds. In forgiveness there are no winners and losers. Everyone's a winner and everyone gets a prize.

The propensity to forgive emerges and matures across the life span. For most people, forgiveness is learned very early in life, and for many, forgiveness is taught within the nuclear family as a way to promote harmony. Even in our public education system we learn that getting along with others depends on the principle of forgiveness. Thus, it is safe to assume that, if queried about forgiveness, no member of society would be unaware of the concept or what it means, although there might be variations with respect to how strongly people believe in the efficacy of forgiveness, as well as where they attribute the source of this principle's practice in their lives.

Positive Agers not only understand the value of forgiveness, but they know how to apply it in everyday living. It is an integral Positive Aging strategy that promotes well-being in old age and, like the other strategies it involves giving and receiving. Good forgivers know not only how to forgive, but they also know the steps that they must take to seek and receive forgiveness (Enright, 2001).

Giving Forgiveness

Across your lifetime you will forgive in many different ways; the most common is toward another person. If someone offends you, you can, through forgiveness, heal your hurt. It is noteworthy that forgiving does not require that the offender acknowledge or even feel sorry for the hurt that he or she has caused. Because the source of forgiveness does not rest with the offender, it is entirely within you to give forgiveness. In fact, you can choose not to forgive even if the offender begs for your forgiveness. This personal feature of forgiveness is what makes it so powerful, that is, you don't have to depend on others before engaging in forgiveness. This is also true for the positive emotional consequences that follow forgiveness. These are naturally occurring emotions that follow the sincere act of forgiving.

In addition to forgiving others, you can also forgive yourself. Everyone makes mistakes and will recall experiencing disappointments, shame, or self-condemnation for failure to achieve a goal, for an error in judgment, or for a harmful act. Errors of this sort can cause you to berate yourself and feel miserable. Research suggests that we are neurologically wired to feel disappointment or self-anger so as to induce us to change our behavior when it goes awry (Transcredi, 2005). However, this kind of self-effacement, if it goes on chronically, can cause serious emotional damage including a lifestyle of negativity and regret. As a central aspect of Positive Aging, self-forgiveness that emerges as a form of self-compassion has been found to produce positive affect and enhanced personal adjustment (Neff, 2003).

As a Positive Ager, practicing self-forgiveness builds insight and understanding about who you are as an imperfect person who lives in an imperfect world where mistakes and problems will occur

(Ingersoll-Dayton & Krause, 2005). In the same vein, you can also learn to forgive Nature or God for acts that have harmed you or others. If a natural disaster occurs and your property is destroyed or a loved one is hurt, you may feel angry toward Mother Nature or God. To feel better toward others, yourself, or in the things that you believe requires that you forgive.

Social scientists have been intensely interested in the role of forgiveness as a cumulative life-span force for better living. The science of forgiveness suggests that forgiving requires a special form of self-reflection which involves a worldview that is not idealized and an approach that underscores compassion. Unforgiving comes from rigid expectations that you may place on others, yourself, or your world (Thoresen, Harris, & Luskin, 2000), and when those expectations are not met, disappointment ensues. Following disappointment, feelings range from mild indignation to rage. A person who is chronically depressed may rehearse such a dynamic many times and will often have difficulty forgiving himself or herself, even for inconsequential events (Maltby, Day, & Barber, 2004). Freedom from this maladaptive thinking not only has mental health benefits, there are positive physical consequences as well. In fact, a growing body of research (Lawler, Younger, Piferi, Jobe, Edmundson, & Jones, 2005) has documented that forgiving reduces the following:

- Chronic anger and its personal corollaries including depression.
- Hostility.
- High blood pressure and cardiovascular reactivity.
- Susceptibility to disease (preserves immune response).
- Negative emotions.

Although forgiveness has not been directly linked to longevity per se, it is fair to reason that it can protect a person from some disease states (such as cardiovascular disease) by diminishing unhealthy processes that result in stress. Practicing a lifestyle of forgiveness will result in an increased capacity to mobilize your emotional resources and to feel and think flexibly about yourself, others, and your world. People who are "good" forgivers tend to focus on the positives, and this in turn works to preserve well-being and the capacity for Positive Aging. Developing a lifestyle pattern of giving forgiveness will help you live better and feel happier during your later years.

Seeking Forgiveness

An important component in the process of forgiving is the seeking of forgiveness. The need to seek forgiveness occurs nearly every day for all people across every conceivable circumstance. For example, if you bump into someone while walking, you might immediately say, "I'm sorry" or "Pardon me" or "Excuse me." These common acknowledgments that a mistake has been made request the receiver of the mistake to not take offense at the wrongful act or the person who committed it.

Consider the last time you were pulled over for a traffic violation. You usually know what you have done wrong and law enforcement is there to acknowledge it. As you sit in your car and the police officer approaches you wish for a miracle and, once in a while, you get your wish. The officer reminds you that you have indeed broken the law, but then says there will be no ticket or fine, just a warning this time. You are forgiven and you feel relief. Life is good. You may feel better after not receiving this ticket than you did before you were pulled over. In gratitude for this act of forgiveness, you might try harder to obey traffic laws in the future.

The process of forgiveness as shown in this example is that you have committed a wrongful act; you have done harm to another person, thing, or yourself. There is acknowledgment that this wrong has been committed and a consequence must be served. However, if you are sorry or show remorse for having committed a wrongful act, you might be able to reconcile the deed through mercy. Mercy is a form of clemency or kindness extended to someone instead of the strictness or severity of justice. Yes, you made a mistake or an error, but forgiveness indicates that mercy has been extended instead of justice.

Although the topic of forgiveness is well known and is easy to grasp intellectually through simple examples in everyday living, it can be very difficult to master, particularly for those offenses that a victim might deem as being more significant or substantial. There are a number of forgiveness processes. The social scientist Robert Enright (2001) uses guideposts or phases to operationalize the steps in forgiveness. These phases are outlined below along with specific markers that characterize each phase. Working through each of these phases results in the receiving of forgiveness.

GUIDEPOSTS FOR SEEKING FORGIVENESS

- Phase I: Uncovering Guilt and Shame
  - Are you ashamed of what you have done?
  - Do you go over and over the event in your mind?
  - Have you denied your guilt or pretended that what you did wasn't harmful?
- Phase II: Deciding to Seek Forgiveness
  - Recognize that when you wrong another person, you should seek forgiveness.
  - Recognize that when another person offers forgiveness, you should be willing to accept it.
- Phase III: Working on Receiving Forgiveness
  - Work toward gratitude.
  - Work toward reconciliation.
  - Work toward humility.
- Phase 4: Discovering
  - Finding meaning in personal failure.
  - Realize that you are not alone.
  - Make a decision to change.

The guideposts process illustrates that seeking forgiveness occurs at two levels. First, an emotional shift occurs when a person realizes that he or she has done something wrong. This is described in Phase I & II. Second, is that the identified act—which is usually labeled as a crime, sin, or wrongdoing—is rectified and then reinterpreted as a source of positive meaning before forgiveness is received. Enright effectively utilized this model of forgiveness in treating women who have been abused sexually as children (Enright, 2001).

For a person to be forgiven she or he must recognize that a wrong has been done, feel remorseful for it, and then rectify it. Doing so provides relief to the victim of the offense and, in the process, removes the wrongful act from the wrongdoer. A Jewish approach to forgiveness is instructive of this process because not only does it articulate each component, it also delineates a pathway for returning to a state of worthiness (or *teshuvah*):

- The wrongdoer must acknowledge committing a wrongful act.
- There must be a public confession of the wrongdoing by the wrongdoer.

- There must also be a public expression of remorse by the wrongdoer.
- The wrongdoer then announces a resolve not to act in this way again.
- There is an observable compensation paid to the victim of equal (or greater value) of the harm done by the wrong deed.
- A sincere request of forgiveness from the victim must be made.
- The wrongdoer must avoid the conditions in the future that caused the initial offense.

Although seeking forgiveness in this way can be difficult, as it requires publicly admitting or acknowledging a wrongful act, the benefits of receiving forgiveness can yield powerful positive emotions for the wrongdoer, whether the act is forgiven by the victim or not.

In the secular literature most practitioners of forgiveness have described steps that one must take to forgive or to be forgiven. Fred Luskin, a psychologist who has advocated for forgiveness as a method for social and individual change, popularized a nine-step intervention (Luskin, 2003), namely, (a) identify your source of anger, (b) commit to do something about it, (c) work on finding inner peace, (d) recognize what needs to be forgiven, (e) prepare yourself to forgive through stress management, (f) let go of expectations about any specific outcome, (g) focus your energy outward and away from hatred, (h) learn to love—not necessarily the wrongdoer, and (i) write a new self-script that acknowledges, but does not focus on, the grievance. Luskin's approach suggests that people can dramatically improve well-being by engaging in this process. The Stanford Northern Ireland Project conducted by Luskin and his colleagues invited women from Ireland who had an immediate family member murdered in the religious conflicts there to Stanford University for a weeklong workshop to learn Luskin's forgiveness model. As these women engaged forgiveness, they experienced diminished hurt and had increased emotional energy for coping. They were then able to take these newly learned skills back to their home country where they became agents of social change to help heal many hurts and wounds that were a result of this conflict.

II. A POSITIVE AGING APPROACH TO FORGIVENESS

Forgiveness is a Positive Aging strategy that is illustrated in the following story about Ray. Ray had a reputation for bearing grudges and not letting go of hurts he had received. In this story, Ray discovers that forgiveness can achieve a desired outcome, and repair relationships.

RAY'S EXPERIENCE WITH FORGIVENESS

Ray, a 70-year-old retiree, and his wife had for 10 years lived in a corner house in a suburban subdivision with covenants forbidding street parking. Previous to this, they owned a condominium downtown near where Ray worked. Ray disliked the condominium because it was close to the street and the noise of cars and the traffic congestion were very noticeable. Once Ray retired they sold the condo and bought their current home, which they believed would give him respite from the annoying city traffic and parking. The new home had large trees that provided privacy. Ray worried that because the home was on a corner lot it might attract cars parking along the curb. The home owners' association insisted that this would not be the case since there was a strict rule against parking on the street. Ray's neighbor, however, did not follow this rule and began parking his motor home in front of Ray's house. At first this occurred infrequently, but over several months the neighbor began leaving his motor home in the street for longer and longer periods of time. When the homeowners' association did not act on Ray's complaints about the motor home, he decided to take matters into his own hands. He began turning on his sprinkling system and directing the heads so that they would spray on his neighbor's motor home. Ray hoped this would discourage his neighbor. Unfortunately, it had the opposite effect by making his neighbor angry and entrenching his behavior even more. Ray and his neighbor exchanged harsh words from across the street. Ray, who was prone to worry, began to lose sleep over this issue. This obsession with the motor home concerned his wife and his five adult children as well. Ray even consented to see a counselor at his wife's urging because she believed that this issue had triggered a depressive episode. He vehemently complained that it was caused by his neighbor's acts.

Ray was an avid television watcher and enjoyed watching Court TV. In one episode the judge suggested to an angry plaintiff that his anger was getting him nowhere and that he should forgive the defendant for her trespass on his property. Ray was intrigued by this suggestion and spoke to his wife about the possibility of acting like he was forgiving his neighbor. She encouraged Ray to not just go through the motions but to really try to reconcile his differences with the neighbor by going across the street and talking with him about it. Ray was angry with his wife for suggesting that he was not sincere in his attempt to forgive his neighbor, and this reminded Ray that over the course of his life he did have a problem with bearing grudges. His wife's encouragement initially made Ray feel even worse and even angrier about the situation. In spite of his mixed feelings, several days later Ray hatched a plan that involved him delivering a fruit basket to the neighbor's porch with a note of apology, ringing the doorbell, then running away. He purchased the basket and went across the street to deliver it. To Ray's surprise, the neighbor (who had watched Ray cross the street) answered the door immediately. Before Ray could say anything, the neighbor screamed at Ray and told him to get off his porch, stated that Ray was "scum," and that he was calling the police. The only thing Ray thought to do was to push the fruit basket into the neighbor's arms and say, "I'm sorry for the problems." Ray then walked away quickly while his neighbor took the fruit basket back into his house. Ray was now an emotional wreck. He hadn't expected his visit to turn out that way. "Forgiveness is worthless," he thought, "and on top of that I'm going to have a nervous breakdown." Interestingly, later that evening he was able to calm down. He slept well that night, although he rehearsed the incident in his mind several times prior to sleep. Ray wondered what was relaxing him. Finally, he concluded that it was this thought: "I did everything I could and now it's finished. I don't need to talk to my neighbor anymore."

Over a period of days Ray quit thinking about the incident, forgot about his neighbor, forgot about the motor home, and moved on with his life. A few weeks later Ray noticed that the motor home was not parked on the street anymore. He thought that the neighbor might be on vacation. On a Saturday morning a month later Ray heard a knock on his door. It was the neighbor. Ray noticed that the neighbor was upset and he asked him what was wrong. The neighbor said that he hadn't been able to get the incident with Ray off of his mind. He couldn't figure out why Ray had given him that fruit basket and had apologized. He had berated himself for acting awful to Ray and for violating the neighborhood covenants. Finally, the neighbor had decided to move his motor home to a storage facility to give Ray some relief and to comply with the rules. So, he said, "I thought I would come over and apologize." Ray was overwhelmed. He had no idea that his apologizing had exerted such an impact. Ray and the neighbor talked a short time about the incident and they both agreed that this issue had been blown out of proportion, and they decided to forgive each other. Over the course of the next few weeks Ray and his neighbor visited frequently and learned more about each other, talked about the neighborhood and discovered that they had many things in common. In fact, Ray was interested in buying a motor home and he and his neighbor went motor home shopping together. From this event a friendship had flourished and Ray and his neighbor continued to spend time together over the next several months. Three days before Christmas Ray suffered a massive stroke and passed away on Christmas morning. The neighbor attended Ray's funeral and pledged to Ray's wife that he would keep a neighborly watch on her and her home as long as they were neighbors.

Ray's experiment in forgiveness demonstrates how it can be a source of positive change even when it is not certain that it will produce the desired results. Ray was a reluctant forgiver; however, he still discovered its power as a Positive Aging strategy for repairing a relationship and reestablishing his well-being. Forgiveness builds Positive Aging characteristics that can, in turn, help you find happiness in old age even when you encounter difficulties. Here are several ways in which forgiveness can be used to foster Positive Aging.

Forgiveness and Mobilizing Resources

It takes a special kind of discipline to forgive, including the ability to change how you routinely think and feel. It is easy to view yourself, your situation, or another person in a resentful way because blaming, feeling victimized, or being taken advantage of places responsibility outside of yourself. Self-statements like the ones below are based on the belief that others are responsible for your well-being:

- I am a victim.
- I hate you for doing this to me.

- You are responsible for my problems.
- I can't do anything about my situation.

When you rehearse these kinds of statements you will find yourself feeling trapped by your own situation. But, how can you alter negative self-statements when they threaten to dominate how you think and feel? The answer to this question is both easy and difficult. It is easy when you realize that these are only verbal statements. They do not dictate your feelings. In fact, they have no power in and of themselves. You are the source of their potency. In essence, by internalizing these statements you rob yourself of your ability to change.

The difficult part is knowing how to feel differently. You might, for example, have very legitimate reasons to justify your situation. Someone may have, indeed, offended you. Your health may have taken an unexpected turn for the worse, or you may have done something wrong. You can't prevent bad things from happening to you. But, you can decide not to allow those "bad things" to disempower you. This is where forgiveness comes in as a way to give yourself permission to feel good, through: (a) acknowledging that something bad has happened, (b) accepting that it occurred because the world is not perfect, but (c) understanding that you are in charge of how you will interpret how you feel about this event, and (d) deciding to choose not to let this negative situation dictate how you feel about yourself. This is how forgiveness transforms internalized negative self-perceptions into thoughts that allow a person to move forward, even in the presence of hurt, mistakes, problems, and difficulties.

In later life, some of those negative events are unavoidable, and even predictable. The older you are, the greater the likelihood that you will acquire a chronic health condition that will impair your function and may even cause you physical pain. To think otherwise would be naïve. However, you are not required to allow circumstances to determine your sense of well-being. Instead, a forgiveness view of a chronic health condition is one that acknowledges that you are physically imperfect, but when those imperfections emerge they will not cause you to lose your positive sense of yourself. This does require some disciplined thinking, but if you practice cultivating a forgiving attitude you will learn to let go of resentment and

122

self-condemnation as challenges arise. Through forgiveness, you can focus on what you are still capable of enjoying, even in the presence of serious personal difficulties.

Forgiveness and Flexibility

Anger and resentment are inflexible patterns of thinking. When you resent another person you almost always experience a desire to seek revenge or retribution. This, of course, sets in motion a self-destructive fixated cycle that can only end in personal disappointment. When you look down this path and realize that there is nothing but misery at the end, it is time to choose another way. Forgiveness can be the alternative option. Strategies that are part of a forgiving response such as reframing resentment, putting aside a grudge, or suspending a judgment all involve a degree of flexibility in thinking. In the example of Ray, he began thinking flexibly when he entertained the idea that he could forgive his neighbor. He shifted his negative judgments about his neighbor's acts in a direction that encouraged reconciliation. At first, Ray was not sure that he was capable of doing this, so he considered simply going through the motions without really allowing himself to get hopeful. However, even though his approach was tentative it contained elements of hope that things could get better. Once Ray allowed himself to do this, he set in motion possibilities for change that ultimately allowed him to find a way out of his dilemma.

Flexibility in how we think, feel, and behave as we grow older is essential to change our view of difficulties when they arise. If you lose a loved one to death, it is no longer possible to hold on to that relationship. Therefore, you must think differently and find new ways to meet old needs. Letting go of the resentment of loss opens the door to this kind of flexible thinking. Positive Agers employ the skill of forgiveness to cultivate hope even when personal circumstances indicate that little hope exists.

Forgiveness as a Positive Life Choice

As you engage in forgiveness, it changes you and shapes your life. This change is manifested in how you view problems or issues. Fears that your problems will overwhelm you and destroy your quality of life can be diminished through forgiveness. This capacity to understand that life is difficult whether it is due to your own actions, your circumstances, or the acts of others, but to accept that this does not mean that you can not be happy, requires interpreting external events in such a way that they do not disrupt your internal sense of satisfaction.

Earlier, the demons of decline were described. They personify loss, and a host of negative transitions associated with advancing age. We all hope to avoid these. However, when they come, they need not determine your happiness. You can still find sources of meaning in living and discover contentment, even though this might involve finding it in the presence of physical pain, suffering, or difficult living circumstances. Forgiveness can be counted on to help you deal with these negatives, because unlike the demons of decline (which you cannot stop or control), forgiveness is entirely under the control of the forgiver (or the person who is sincerely seeking forgiveness). If you seek forgiveness and someone refuses to forgive you, you still benefit from the action you took. You will find peace of mind in the present even when loss occurs. It does not matter whether your sincere act of forgiveness is rebuffed or ignored or accepted by others. Your effort to forgive helps you to let go of feelings of guilt or anger towards problems. Forgiveness helps you and, secondarily, it benefits others. This is why individuals who learn how to develop a life pattern of forgiveness inevitably learn to find peace of mind regardless of what befalls them.

Forgiveness as a Way to Focus on the Positives

Negativity and anger entrench people in their problems. Forgiveness can help you reframe your difficulties in a positive light. This does not mean that all problems have a silver lining, or that you will not struggle to address a difficult issue, but it does mean that through forgiveness you have a source of framing problems that yields an outcome which enhances, rather than detracts, from your well-being. Many problems that are a result of growing old can be opportunities to apply coping skills to find new sources of meaning. Optimistically looking for those meaning sources is what forgiveness is all about.

As you engage in forgiveness, it changes you and shapes your life. This change comes in how you view problems or issues. Your fears that problems will overwhelm you and affect your quality of life will diminish because your source of well-being does not come from fighting off problems, but from letting go of the imperfections of the world. Viewing problems as opportunities is embedded in a forgiveness approach. This does not mean that all problems will be solved or that you won't struggle to address issues, but it does mean that you have a source of reframing a problem in such a way that it yields an outcome that enhances rather than takes away from your well-being. Problems are not threats to be avoided or challenged; they are opportunities to apply coping skills to address them—such as through forgiveness—and in the process you grow and mature and discover new sources of well-being.

A person who is expert at forgiving does not give up the right to have justice, needs, or pleasures, or to experience peace of mind or the "good life" in any shape or form. On the contrary, practicing forgiveness enhances your ability to enjoy the good things in life. Our imperfect world will challenge us in both positive and negative directions. A forgiving person does not try to change or punish other people or things. People can only change themselves, and others will act according to laws and/or circumstances.

Imagine a person you know who consistently makes affirmative life choices, and you will discover someone who knows how to forgive. Such a person is rarely a victim even though that person may have faced devastating losses or have been subjected to harsh treatment. Perpetual victims focus on their problems and are trapped by them. They cannot move on. Moving on takes effort and a life focused on the present. Forgiveness helps a person to do this.

With the challenges that are presented in old age, a forgiving lifestyle is particularly important. You can't stop age-related decline, you can't prevent losses, you will not be able to turn back the clock and relieve chronic pain, disease, or even your own impending death, so you must learn to accept these aspects of yourself and your world that are realistically unchangeable. Engaging forgiveness fosters life patterns that will influence how you feel about others as well as how others feel about you. To develop a lifestyle that is motivated by forgiveness keep these concepts in mind:

- Seeking and giving forgiveness is, first, for you and secondarily for others.
- Forgiveness is primarily a way of thinking and secondarily a behavior.

125

- You can forgive and feel better in any situation.
- Forgiveness always helps you move on.

FORGIVENESS EXERCISE

Try this experiment with forgiveness and applying the four ideas outlined above. Take a moment and identify an issue that is bothering you and that you might address with forgiveness. This could be by forgiving someone or something. It could also be through the seeking of forgiveness.

I've reworded the four ideas above as questions. Respond to these as they relate to the issue you have written down.

1. Question #1: How will seeking (or giving) forgiveness help me
2. Question #2: How do I need to think about this issue for me to engage a forgiveness response?
3. Question #3: How will giving (or seeking) forgiveness cause me to feel better?
4. Question #4: How will forgiveness help me to move past this issue?

III. FORGIVENESS AND BEREAVEMENT

Bereavement research has found that selective thinking about the positive characteristics of a loved one helps to ease the grief of the loss. Bonnano (2002) has posited that it may be critical to preserve those positive thoughts and feelings even if one moves on into a new relationship by letting go of negativity surrounding the loss of a loved one. The following example illustrates this.

SARA AND MIKE'S LAST CONVERSATION

Sara is 87 years old and is haunted by the fact that the day before her husband unexpectedly died they had engaged in a bitter argument. Sara had wanted to drive out to see her daughter the upcoming week for her daughter's birthday. Sara's husband Bill, on the other hand, preferred to fly their daughter to their home and celebrate their daughter's birthday in their home. Although Sara's daughter was willing to celebrate her birthday either way, both Sara and Bill were determined, as Sara noted, "to have their way." Unfortunately, their argument went on into the evening and they went to bed upset at each other. During the night, Bill died in his sleep of a heart attack. Sara was horrified by this event and blamed herself for precipitating her husband's death. She was unable to stop grieving until she decided enough is enough and that she needed to forgive herself. To do so, she engaged the following steps:

- *First, she reframed the event positively. Their argument was a sign that they had a healthy and happy marriage. She wasn't afraid to tell Bill what she thought.*
- *Second, an argument did not mean that Bill no longer loved Sara. Even in the best marriages there are arguments.*
- *Third, if Bill were still alive he would certainly forgive her. He would not want her to suffer.*

Finding positive affect when there is no opportunity to realistically right a wrong or fix a problem is an invaluable skill. To do so harnesses psychological forces underlying forgiveness to heal you even when circumstances won't change. In this story the "shoulds" or "what ifs" are almost guaranteed to move a person toward the negative: "If I would have done this . . ." Such phrases mean that you can't forgive yourself and, as a result, you are left with the loss or the problem. Employing forgiveness, which helps you to focus on the positives, puts the past into the past and allows you to focus on what is good or happy about the present. This brings peace of mind.

Chapter 7

STRATEGY #7: YOU CAN POSSESS
A GRATEFUL ATTITUDE

I. GRATITUDE

"Count your blessings."

This is a ubiquitous admonition that can be found in one form or another in every religious tenant, East and West. But just what does it mean to "count your blessings"? The message here is that you should be thankful for (or appreciate) the benefits you have received from living. Cultivating a grateful attitude is not only a basic element for happiness in life, but it facilitates adaptation in almost every social system. Patrick Fitzgerald (1998) underscored three elements of gratitude: (1) a warm sense of appreciation for somebody or something, (2) a sense of goodwill toward that person or thing, and (3) a desire to act based upon this sense of goodwill toward another.

Gratitude is a developmental construct. As children, we learn about gratitude in our families of origin and in our schools. We are exposed to gratitude in the workplace and among our friends and neighbors. Gratitude not only makes life a little easier, but it is a powerful strategy for coping with the challenges and difficulties that arise in everyday living. Melody Beattie, an author and philosopher, described gratitude as the ultimate reframing technique to turn what is ambiguous or questionable into something that has positive meaning. Beattie noted that gratitude:

> unlocks the fullness of life. It turns what we have into enough, and more. It turns denial into acceptance, chaos into order, confusion into clarity. . . . It turns problems into gifts, failures into success, the unexpected into perfect timing, and mistakes into important events. Gratitude makes sense of our past, brings peace for today, and creates a vision for tomorrow. (p. 25)

Gratitude is an inherently human emotion that involves feelings of appreciation and thankfulness. The best descriptions of how gratitude works are some of the simplest. The traditions and stories of indigenous people such as the following from the North American Inuit (or Eskimo) Tribe (Millman, 1987) underscores this fact:

TIGGAK

There was a man named Tiggak whose only son drowned in the sea. And such a powerful grief came to the old man that he set up his hut right next to his son's grave. The very first night he was awakened by noises. An ice-bear, a walrus, a hare, and a fox were busy removing the stones from the grave. Tiggak was furious and threatened them with his spear.

- *"But how do you think that we get our teeth?" said the fox.*
- *"How do you think that we got our whiskers?" the walrus said.*
- *"And how do you think we got our (vital organs)?" the hare said.*
- *"We must perforce steal from the dead," declared the ice-bear.*

Whereupon Tiggak allowed them to take whatever they wanted from his son. The grateful animals repaid his kindness many times over, for there wasn't a day after that when he didn't have good hunting. (p. 184)

This legend illustrates that gratitude generates positive emotions. It is linked to kindness as well as other affirmative feelings like joy, wonder, awe, and appreciation. These can be applied to cultivate resources to deal with the challenges of living. Adults who have refined the skill of being grateful know how to find well-being in old age. Gratitude helps people to deal with loss and disappointment, including irreversible loss such as the death of a loved one.

As a personal act that has received careful empirical study by psychologists and social scientists, gratitude has been documented as a cognitive strategy that can be employed to mediate unhappiness and challenge negative emotional states like resentment, regret, and envy (Roberts, 2004).

Philosophers like Aafke Komter (2004) have used the metaphor of gift exchange to describe how gratitude works. When someone gives you a gift, if the giver of the gift is sincere, it sends you the message that you are worth enough for the giver to extend some of his or her finite resources to you. This could include tangible gifts like your personal time, physical resources, material items, or anything meaningful that is under the control of the gift giver. This is why the receiver often says thank you, expressing gratitude to the gift giver. If you feel gratitude toward the giver then the giver means something to you. The receiver usually assesses not only the gift, but the giver, and an emotional experience follows that strengthens relationship bonds.

This example of gift giving highlights characteristics of gratitude:

- The giving of a gift to a receiver
- The receiver valuing the gift
- The receiver evaluating the giver in relation to the gift
- An emotional response that is generated in the receiver called *gratitude*

These steps underscore that although humans have the propensity to experience gratitude, it is, like the other meaning-centered strategies, learned and cultivated over the life span. Ralph Marston, a motivational speaker and self-help author, asked:

> What if you gave someone a gift, and they neglected to thank you for it—would you be likely to give them another? Life is the same way. In order to attract more of the blessings that life has to offer, you must appreciate what you already have. (http://www.brainyquote.com/quotes/r/ralphmarst132943.html)

Self-help books and Internet sites are replete with strategies that a person can employ to feel more grateful. Most of these involve generating gratitude by explicitly acknowledging things or people for which one is grateful. An exercise that has been tested in the psychological sciences and found to have value in promoting positive emotions is "gratitude journaling." Beginning a gratitude journal is quite simple and its goals are straightforward: to create a positive mind-set by recording grateful thoughts on a daily basis. In one study conducted by Robert Emmons and Michael McCollough (2003), two social scientists who have extensively studied the adaptive qualities of gratitude, they proposed a gratitude journaling intervention with the following instructions provided to the study participants:

> There are many things in our lives, both large and small, that we might be grateful about. Think back over the past week and write down on the lines below up to five things in your life that you are grateful or thankful for. (p. 388)

In the Emmons & McCollough study, those persons who engaged in gratitude journaling showed better well-being on measures of self-esteem and life satisfaction. These researchers concluded that inducing feelings of gratitude through journaling was more successful in generating positive emotional feelings than two control groups that consisted of participants who kept journals that did not focus on gratitude.

Suggestions for cultivating a sense of gratitude are highlighted below and these can be used by anyone at any age.

GRATITUDE JOURNALING

- Make a gratitude journal. Record your thoughts during the day about your daily experiences in a grateful way (reflecting on things that make you smile, bring you happiness or joy, or make you feel at peace).
  - Set a minimum number of entries per day (e.g., no fewer than 5) and increase the number of entries per week, up to 15, as you get better at noticing things for which you are grateful.
- Recollect what you have felt grateful for in the past. How have these things positively influenced your everyday living?

- Realize that the world is "not perfect" but you can be grateful no matter what condition you are in. For example,
  - You can be grateful whether you are sick or healthy. If you are sick, you may choose to be grateful for the times that you feel good. If you are not sick, you can be grateful for your good health.
  - You can be grateful in difficult situations. In such instances gratitude may not solve your problem, but it can help you find positives even when they may not be apparent. If you have been in an accident, you can be grateful that you survived it. You can also be grateful for the things that you have left versus those things that you have lost.
  - You can be grateful in the presence of loss. For example, the death of a loved one is a profoundly sorrowful event. However, statements like "I am grateful for the time we had together" or "He/she lived a long and healthy life" can negate emotions such as anger, sorrow, blame, guilt, and shame.

Gratitude is a very accessible Positive Aging strategy since it primarily involves shifting your state of mind from one valence (negative) to another (positive). It does take practice and repetition in order for it to become a natural reaction to a negative life challenge. And, what is powerful about gratitude is that you don't even need to engage in any physical behavior or even lift a finger to generate feelings of gratitude. You can do it all in your head.

To demonstrate this, sit back in your chair for a moment. Close your eyes. Recollect the best thing that happened to you during the past week. Take a minute and pay attention to those feelings that were associated with this positive event. Are you grateful for the event? Assuming that you are, you can dwell on the reasons that you feel grateful. As you practice this simple exercise for just a few minutes, you will notice that your affect will change in a positive direction and not just about the event, but for other things as well. You may feel that "It's great to be alive" or "Good things happen to me."

Although it is easy to generate gratitude in a neutral situation, or when things are going well, applying gratitude to difficult life-span transitions can be even more challenging if you do not have routines that include gratitude. This kind of challenge is highlighted in the vignette that follows:

RICHARD'S CHALLENGING INTERACTION

Richard is a 69-year-old retiree who returned to school to get a second bachelor's degree in English. It was not long before he found himself struggling in several of his university classes. In one class in particular, his professor made a number of negative comments on a paper he had written and the professor indicated that Richard needed to do some remedial work on his writing skills. The professor even went so far as to suggest that Richard consider going to the campus counseling center to seek some guidance regarding the poor attitude Richard had developed toward the class. Richard, a professionally oriented person who worked for years as a technical writer, was dumbfounded by this suggestion. He did, however, make an appointment with a counselor to discuss what he described as his problem with how to deal with an unreasonable and narrow-minded professor. For two sessions, Richard complained about the professor and his dislike of him, both in the classroom and when he got feedback about his papers. One of the interventions the counselor recommended that Richard engage in was a gratitude journal. *Specifically, the counselor suggested that Richard begin to think about reasons he was grateful to be attending this particular English class. Richard followed the counselor's advice and soon began to report that, although the class was difficult and he didn't agree with the professor, there was still much to be learned in this class. He was particularly grateful for his fellow students who were always supportive when Richard presented his work orally. Richard also reported that he was grateful to be learning to write differently than he had practiced while working in industry and that he was impressed with how different the writing was in an academic context. Soon, Richard began to report enjoying attending the class and even challenging the professor a time or two. He noted, "If I ever challenged my boss with new ideas, he would have fired me; however, even if the professor disagrees with my point of view, it always ends up becoming an interesting classroom discussion."*

This story highlights the power of cultivating a grateful attitude. The steps that Richard took to deal with this situation were as follows:

- Letting go of his sense of entitlement about writing.
- Placing positive value on his learning experience by being grateful for the opportunity to learn.
- Reframing his animosity toward the professor by changing his assumptions about the professor's motivations.
- Having fun with the experience and diminishing its seriousness.
- Building his self-confidence through thinking thoughts about himself consistent with gratitude ("I can come up with new ideas").

These are the underlying themes in developing a grateful attitude, namely, (a) finding (or creating) a positive mind-set, (b) valuing yourself and the experience—good or bad, (c) diminishing the seriousness of the negative event, and (d) building your self-confidence. As you cultivate strong gratitude skills, they will protect you against the instances in your life when injustice occurs or when you feel that you are wronged. Gratitude is a flexible strategy because it can address almost any issue.

II. POSITIVE AGING AND GRATITUDE

Of the Positive Aging strategies, gratitude, like forgiveness, is a reframing technique. Because gratitude and misery are incompatible—that is, you cannot be grateful and miserable simultaneously—people who have experienced difficulties in life or are confronting a challenge or obstacle can keep up a positive mood and thereby generate resources for coping by simply practicing thinking grateful thoughts. Like the other Positive Aging strategies, the ability to engage in grateful thinking is a skill that requires practice. The four Positive Aging characteristics can be employed to learn the skill of being grateful. As you become better at using gratitude to address challenges, you will strengthen these Positive Aging characteristics in the process.

Mobilizing Resources for Gratitude

Gratitude does not occur in a vacuum, and it requires effort to be grateful, especially when circumstances are such that it is easy to dwell on the negative. When you experience a loss, a setback, or a tragedy, it is almost natural to focus on the negative. If you do so, one of the consequences of that focus is the magnification of the loss.

Cognitive shifting is the element of gratitude that helps you move your thoughts about a difficulty or a tragedy from the negative to the positive. To do this you must discipline yourself to focus on what you "have" instead of what you "don't have." This involves letting go of negative emotions that keep you attached to set backs. It is fair to say that almost everyone has experienced disappointment at one time or another, and the process of recovering from a challenge or tragedy can be not only time-consuming but infuriating as well, particularly the more blame we place on ourselves or others who we construe as responsible for a difficult circumstance. In the following example, I experienced this challenge and was able use gratitude to "put right" negative emotions associated with a loss.

MY STOLEN BRIEFCASE

Recently my briefcase was stolen from my office due to an error that I made. After arriving one morning for work, I placed my briefcase under my desk in my office and left to meet with a colleague whose office was just around the corner. I neglected to lock my door when I left, only to find, when I returned after being away less than half an hour, that someone had walked into my office and nabbed my briefcase. It had contained my computer, my wallet including checks and credit cards, my Palm Pilot, and my teaching materials. It was a tough loss and my first instinct was to feel animosity toward the thief and to focus on all the items in my briefcase that I no longer had in my possession. I berated myself for leaving my door unlocked and then wondered how I would ever replace all of those things. To make matters worse, less than two hours later I discovered that someone was using my credit cards fraudulently. So I spent the remainder of the day canceling my credit cards, closing bank accounts, replacing my driver's license, and obtaining a new university identification card, library card, and recreation card. It seemed to me that my entire life was tucked away in the various pockets of that briefcase. The effort to recapture all of these items was daunting. This would be a time-consuming task in my already busy life. My computer and the files stored on it would not be easily recovered. Even though I knew that my briefcase was gone, I still hoped that I would find the discarded case somewhere, that the thieves might have been kind enough to at least leave the briefcase for me to salvage. I wandered the building for some time, looking in trash cans and in corners for my case. It was, of course, not to be found. Then I reached in my pocket and noticed my car keys. For some reason, I had not placed them in my briefcase, as was my typical routine. I stopped for a moment and shifted my thinking to gratitude that I still had those keys. I noticed as I held the keys tightly in my hand that I was immediately feeling better about the overall situation. These keys would have been another item to replace, especially my car keys. With this added boost of emotional energy, I decided that I would replace all this "stuff," but at least I wouldn't need to replace my keys because today I had been lucky.

This is how gratitude works, but it takes some effort to shift your focus from what you have "lost" to what you have "left." The ending to this tragedy came as I slowly replaced all of my stolen possessions. Today, I hardly remember the theft. Most of my lost goods were replaceable and those that weren't were ultimately forgotten. This story is a small example of how gratitude mobilizes psychological resources. However, gratitude also works for more significant instances, including the loss of one's health, the loss of a home, and even the loss of a lifelong partner. Gratitude does not objectively replace your losses, but it provides an alternative way to think about them that allows you to generate resources for coping. I have designed the "Reframing Regrets" exercise to help you learn how the emotional valence–shifting aspect of gratitude works.

REFRAMING REGRETS

Identify something in your life that you currently regret, that is, something in the past that you wish you would have done differently. This regret can be big or small. It might involve another person or it may simply involve you. Write that regret down in the space provided below. I have listed an example to help you get started.

Describe a regret.

Example: I regret not finding more time to be with my grandson when he was very young. Now he has little interest in me.

_____

_____

_____

Reframe your regret. Using the example above, you could reason, "But I am grateful for the time that I *did* spend with him" or "My grandson and I still have time to cultivate a relationship." This grateful reframing puts a positive twist on the regret, thereby nullifying much of its negative emotional impact. You focus on what is good about the memory and these "good thoughts" replace negative reminiscence. In addition to making this affirmative statement, you can strengthen it further by focusing on the times that you have spent with your grandson. You might review photos you have of these times to generate positive emotions from your memories. If you succeed in engaging in this kind of grateful affirmation, your mind will naturally move to those positive times that you spent with your grandson and you will experience a general sense of well-being about yourself as well as a good feeling about your grandson. These positive emotions can then be translated into motivation to initiate more contact with your grandson. As you follow this line of thinking, you will have generated emotional energy to act on your thoughts.

To continue with this exercise, reframe the regret you stated above into a positive gratitude statement in the space below.

Change your regret into an opportunity.

Example: There is no time like the present to interact with my grandson and make our relationship better.

_____

_____

Gratitude can be a useful tool for dealing with one of the biggest challenges we can experience in life, the loss of a loved one to death. Research in grief and bereavement has identified the ability to generate positive features of the lost loved one or aspects of the relationship of which one is grateful for as a way to mediate feelings of loss.

Stroebe, Hansson, Stroebe, and Henk (2001) reinforced the efficacy of grateful memories of a past relationship that ended in death as a source for the survivor's coping in the future. As you make a concerted effort to generate grateful thoughts, they will give you added resources to continue to reap the benefits of living.

Developing a Life Pattern of Gratitude

If practice makes you better at being grateful, then sustained practice can work to establish a life pattern of gratitude. It is easier to be grateful when you persist at it and find new ways to engage in feeling grateful. If you do this, gratitude will become a natural part of your life routine. I'm certain that you've met people who express gratitude frequently. I recall meeting a 72-year-old woman who was attending an AARP lecture that I was giving in a small rural town in eastern Utah. This woman was in a wheelchair and her daughter was with her. She had severe emphysema that she had acquired after many years of cigarette smoking. She was now a nonsmoker. So, in some ways, her behaviors in the past had created problems for her in the present and had taken life away from her in the future. I thought that this woman would be an unlikely candidate for gratitude. I spoke with her briefly after the lecture and she shared with me this thought:

> Dr. Hill, I was a smoker for many years and now I'm paying the price for it. Even so, I'm glad I came to my senses when I was in my 60s and quit smoking because the doctors told me that if I didn't quit, I would surely die within five years. It has been over seven years now and I'm grateful I'm still around and that my body could withstand my cigarette smoking from the past. I also learned a valuable lesson and am a good example to my children and grandchildren about the importance of living right and stopping bad habits before they get the best of you. I'm planning to live another 10 years and I hope to become a great-grandmother before I pass away.

This woman was a Positive Ager. Even though there were many reasons that she could be pessimistic about her future—her condition would only get worse—she found positive meaning in her present. It was unusual to see this manifestation of gratitude in an individual whose choices had caused her health problems; however, it illustrates that it is not necessary for a person to be living an optimal life or making all the right choices for gratitude to work.

An aspect of a grateful attitude is the tendency to expect things to work out in the future. Optimism is an emergent trait that comes from gratitude. Malcolm Cowley (1980) provided a compelling example of the grateful lifestyle by quoting from the famous Catholic poet Paul Claudel, who wrote in his old age:

> Eighty years old! . . . No eyes left, no ears, no teeth, no legs, no wind! And when all is said and done, how astonishingly well one does without them! (p. 17)

Gratitude is an important adaptive quality to acquire as one moves into very late life when, from a practical point of view, it would seem that aging portends misery, not happiness. One might contend that grateful optimism is naive; however, the alternative in very old age, when age-related decline takes away our vitality and capability, is likely misery. If you reach the point in life, toward its end, when you have few resources left, a sense of gratitude can be a great source for positive meaning. Gratitude can help you make that cognitive shift to allow you to deal with the irreconcilables of old age and impending death.

Flexibility and Gratitude

An attribute of gratitude is that it shifts your focus from a fixated set of negative thoughts to thinking more broadly and positively about a situation or an event. It is common to get stuck in a loop of thinking from which breaking out becomes difficult. So why do people sometimes concentrate on a single idea? It may be that such preoccupation has some adaptive purpose. For instance, if you are trying to achieve a goal, then focusing on it may sustain your motivation. In this sense focus or fixation is adaptive. When you focus on something you become attuned to it; you think about it, talk about it, and desire it. If you are focused, you are not likely to be distracted. Fixation is a form of focus that is future oriented. The present becomes less meaningful because your interests are in obtaining a future goal or reward. Great achievements are credited to people who cultivate this kind of focus.

Fixation can also work against you, however, if you fixate on something that you cannot achieve or that is harming you. Setting unachievable goals is sure to be disappointing. For example, not everyone can become a professional athlete, make millions of dollars, or own expensive cars. An unrealistic fixation will also diminish your ability to live in the present. The more unrealistic your fixation, the more power it has to make your present circumstances seem valueless. You might look around at your current situation and feel discouraged with what you have. Your spouse may be letting you down, your job may be unsatisfying, your salary inadequate, your appearance unappealing. All of these types of fixations breed disappointment and are a product of rigid thinking that is also future focused.

When you fixate on something you obsess over it whether it is reasonable or not. Misery can come from this kind of rigid thinking and behaving. Are there ways to break this cycle?

This is where gratitude can be helpful. The scientific literature on gratitude labels it as a reconstrual process that is present focused. Gratitude focuses your thinking and feeling in the present, the here and now. You can be grateful for your ability to play sports, for your spouse, for your job, and for the things that you have. If you follow the admonitions that come from teachers of gratitude (who may be parents, religious leaders, instructors in school) then you must closely examine what you have in the present with the goal of finding positive meaning in it. You might look at your spouse and see a loyal companion or some aspect of his or her physical appearance that generates positive emotions in you. If you do this, you will begin to feel content in the present. Gratitude is a flexibility tool to help you break fixation cycles.

Gratitude and a Positive Focus

In an Internet survey of over 110,000 respondents, researchers Park, Peterson, and Seligman (2005) asked the respondents to endorse strategies that were associated with positive emotions. Gratitude was one of the more frequently noted strategies that they found associated with positive feelings about life and living. If you cultivate a grateful disposition, you will tend to focus on the positives that life has to offer. Rabbi Harold Kushner, author of the best-selling book, *When Bad Things Happen to Good People* (Kushner, 1994), wrote:

> If you concentrate on finding what is good in every situation, you will discover that your life will suddenly be filled with gratitude, a feeling that nurtures the soul. (p. 101)

This highlights the connection between gratitude and positive feelings, which are inextricably bound together. If you want someone to feel good, you admonish them to think about things for which they are grateful. At the same time, if you are feeling good, it is often because you have a sense of appreciation for what you have or what you are experiencing. George Valliant, in describing several of the his participants from the Harvard Study of Adult Development (Valliant, 2002), noted

> Anthony Pirelli is a model of how to grow old, and suggested that aging well has something to do with forgiveness, gratitude, and joy . . . he [Perelli] shows cheerful tolerance of the indignities of old age. He acknowledges and gracefully accepts his dependency needs. When ill, he is a patient for whom a doctor enjoys caring and remembers to be grateful. Whenever possible he turns life's lemons into lemonade. (p. 310)

For Positive Agers, gratitude plays an essential role in reframing the unavoidable challenges of old age, making them meaningful by extracting the positive out of the negative.

III. GRATITUDE AND MANAGING THE CHALLENGES OF LATE-LIFE DOWNSIZING

Late life can be a time of transition. The list of challenges can be long, including dealing with chronic disease, losing family and friends to death, decline, and one's own death. Changes in your living situation as you struggle to cope with declining function in old age is perhaps one of the bigger issues you will encounter, partly because your home is a powerful source of continuity and memories. Home is full of routines that you have developed to make living life easier and more tolerable. Moving out of your home can be a discontinuity even when it is clear that, due to age-related disablement, living in one's home is no longer possible. The following story is an example of how gratitude reaffirmed an older adult's transition to an assisted living setting.

BETTY'S ADJUSTMENT TO SENIOR LIVING

I visited with an older woman named Betty who was living in an assisted care community. She had been living in this facility for over a year when she became consumed by the idea that she wanted to return to the home where she had lived prior to moving to the facility. Her home had been sold when she moved, so it was impossible to objectively address her wish. In her prior home, Betty had lived alone for many years after her husband died. Betty had lived in this home and neighborhood for nearly all of her adult life. She retained vivid memories of her experiences in that home. As Betty became older and more physically frail, she lost her ability to maintain her home and to be safe living alone. In fact, the decision to move her into an assisted care facility had been made after she cut her hands severely while washing dishes. When Betty first made the move, she was quite content in her new surroundings. She liked the company of others in the facility and was relieved that she no longer had to cook her own meals. When a new resident moved in and began complaining about the center and insisting on going home, Betty became disturbed and found fault with her apartment, with others around her, and with the meals she was receiving. All of this combined to make her miserable in her current surroundings. A staff social worker visited with Betty to determine if Betty could let go of her desire to return home. After visiting with Betty it was clear that it would be difficult to deter her from her desire to return home. As an intervention, the social worker suggested that Betty list the things in her old home that she missed. Some of the things on her list included the furnishings in her home, including a couch that she had cherished. The social worker contacted Betty's family and found that they still had this couch. It was decided that the couch would be moved into Betty's apartment to replace her current couch. Betty was comforted by this couch and the memories that it held for her. Interestingly, once the couch had been moved in, Betty found a comb that she had lost many years ago hidden between the couch cushions. Betty's attitude improved and the social worker encouraged

Betty to find ways to think about her life in the assisted living center as a kind of an extension of her previous home. The social worker continued talking with Betty about her previous home and aspects of it that she remembered that brought her positive meaning. From time to time the social worker, with the help of Betty's family, would introduce small items from Betty's home and then allow Betty the opportunity to practice expressing her memories associated with this object (e.g., a mirror, a hat stand, a painting) and why she was grateful for it. As therapy advanced, the social worker was able to take pictures of Betty's previous house and the family who now lived in it. She encouraged Betty to express gratitude that her house was now filled with a happy family who enjoyed it immensely. Over time, Betty lost her desire to leave the assisted living center and began, again, to rediscover the positives of living there and to affirm her decision to transition out of her home.

Although the capacity for gratitude is within all of us, the challenge is finding ways to invoke it. To think that gratitude is a naive mechanism that simply allows you to ignore the challenges and difficulties in life suggests that it is not fully understood. Some things will not change. We need strategies and techniques to deal with the vicissitudes of growing old. If you are truly grateful, you will not ignore reality, but you will be skilled at finding meaning in the "good and the bad" that you encounter.

Epilogue

PUTTING THE SEVEN STRATEGIES FOR POSITIVE AGING TOGETHER

Seven Strategies for Positive Aging involves discrete principles, techniques, and admonitions, in a convenient structure: seven chapters for seven strategies. This organization makes for easy understanding and adoption by you the reader. The ideas are straightforward and little synthesis is required. There are some limitations, however, to this format and questions may remain, including:

- Which strategy should I use when I encounter this or that problem?
- Are some strategies better than others?
- What happens if I try to apply more than one strategy to a problem at any given time?

These questions arise because in real life, problems are not simply solved by matching up a strategy with a particular issue. If you lose a spouse or a loved one to death or if you are the caregiver for a lifetime partner who is suffering from dementia, a single one-size-fits-all approach doesn't always apply. While writing this book, I confronted the issue of how I could present these ideas in such a way as to convey to the reader that these strategies are most effective when they are employed in concert with one another.

Even though each strategy has great merit in its own right, they are best when used together (Hill & Mansour, 2008); people who put these strategies together are models of Positive Aging. If you are engaged in the learning process, it might be enhanced if you also employ gratitude to accentuate the meaning of your learning experiences. If you are forgiven of an act, you often feel grateful for the person who has forgiven you. These examples show that it is overly simplistic to think that you can match one strategy to solve one problem. Furthermore, one strategy does not work for every issue or problem.

If you think of each strategy as a note on a piano, then you realize that each strategy, by itself, might have "tonal" value, that is, the note "C" is a beautiful sound in its own right, but if each strategy is a different key on the piano, the power of the strategies is in playing the notes together versus singly. In fact, if you play the notes in groups, you discover chords that are sounds that amplify the beauty of a single note. Furthermore, if you play all of the notes according to a larger score, then the notes become music that is profoundly more beautiful and enjoyable than a single note or a single chord. It is, of course, more difficult to play music than to simply play notes or chords, so engaging in these strategies as a response set requires more skill.

Consider these strategies as a set of coping skills that can compliment and enhance one another. To review, the seven strategies of Positive Aging are:

- You can find meaning in old age.
- You're never too old to learn.
- You can use the past to cultivate wisdom.
- You can strengthen life-span relationships.
- You can promote growth through giving and receiving help.
- You can forgive yourself and others.
- You can possess a grateful attitude.

Take a moment and identify someone in your life who embodies these characteristics. How did that person acquire these? How does that person employ the strategies as a response set? In Chapter 3 wisdom was introduced. Here, at the end of the book, I want to re-emphasize this term as a label that captures human behavior informed and guided by the seven strategies. Individuals who are able to find well-being in life use these strategies in concert. They know how to learn, how to find meaning, how to change their behavior for the better, how to strengthen life relationships, how to help others, forgive, and feel grateful. They also understand that it takes practice, effort, failure, and even suffering to create a life routine that optimizes coping in old age. This kind of person possesses the characteristics of Positive Aging in that he or she knows how to mobilize resources, act flexibly, make affirmative life decisions, and emphasize the positives that are both a product and an outcome of employing the seven strategies. This is what Positive Aging is and how it works. By utilizing the seven strategies of Positive Aging, you will find ways to discover your potential and cultivate Positive Aging so that you can join those who are finding fulfillment and meaning in growing old.

REFERENCES

Aaronson, B. S. (1960). A dimension of personality change with aging. *Journal of Clinical Psychology, 16*, 63–65.

American Association of Retired Persons. (2002). "The Grandparent Study." Washington, DC. http://research.aarp.org.

Antonucci, T. C., & Akiyama, H. (1987). Social networks in adult life and a preliminary examination of the convoy model. *Journal of Gerontology, 42*, 519–527.

Atchley, R. (1999). *Continuity and adaptation in aging: Creating positive experiences*. Baltimore, MD: Johns Hopkins University Press.

Ball, K., Berch, D. B., Helmers, K. F., Jobe, J. B., Leveck, M. D., et al. (2002). Effects of cognitive training interventions with older adults: A randomized controlled trial. *Journal of the American Medical Association, 288*, 2271–2281.

Baltes, P. B. (1993). The aging mind: Potential and limits. *Gerontologist, 33*, 581–594.

Baltes, P. B. (1997). On the incomplete architecture of human ontogeny: Selection, optimization, and compensation as foundation of developmental theory. *American Psychologist, 52*, 366–380.

Baltes, P. B., Staudinger, U. M., & Lindenberger, U. (1999). Lifespan psychology: Theory and application to intellectual functioning. *Annual Review of Psychology, 50*, 471–507.

Baumeister, R. F., and Leary, M. R. (1995). The need to belong: Desire for interpersonal attachment as a fundamental human motivation. *Psychological Bulletin, 117*, 497–529.

Baumeister, K. F., & Twenge, J. M. (2003). "The social self." In T. Millon & M. J. Lerner (Eds.), *Handbook of psychology: Personality and social psychology.* (vol. 5, pp 327–352). New York: John Wiley.

Beattie, M. (2007). *Gratitude: Inspirations by Melody Beattie, author of The Language of Letting Go.* Hazelden: Center City, MN.

Begley, S. (2007). The upside of aging. *Wall Street Journal,* pp. W1–W4.

Boerner, K., Wortman, C. B., Bonanno, G. A. (2005). Resilient or at risk? A 4-year study of older adults who initially showed high or low distress following conjugal loss. *Journal of Gerontology: Psychological Sciences,* 60B, 67–73.

Bonanno, G. A., Wortman, C. B., Lehman, D. R., Tweed, R. G., Haring, M., Sonnega, J., et al., (2002). Resilience to loss and grief: A prospective study from preloss to 18-months postloss. *Journal of Personality and Social Psychology, 83(5),* 1150–1164.

Camp, C. J. (2006). Montessori-based activities for persons with dementia. Myers Research Institute.

Carnegie, D. (1950). *How to win friends and influence people.* New York: Simon & Schuster.

Carr, D., Nesse, R. M., & Wortman, C. B. (Eds.). (2005). *Spousal bereavement in late life.* New York: Springer.

Corporation for National and Community Service (2007). Keeping baby boomers volunteering. Washington, DC, March.

Cowley, M. (1980). *The view from 80.* New York: Viking Press.

Crown, S. M., & Heron, A. (1965). Psychological aspects of ageing in man. *Annual Review of Psychology, 16,* 417–450.

Dulin, P., Hill, R. D., Anderson, J., & Rasmussen, D. (2001). Altruism as a predictor of life satisfaction in a sample of low-income older adult service providers. *Journal of Mental Health and Aging, 7,* 349–360.

Ellis, S. J. (1990). *By the people: A history of Americans as volunteers.* San Francisco: Jossey-Bass.

Emmons, R. A., & McCullough, M. E. (2003). Counting blessings versus burdens: An experimental investigation of gratitude and subjective well-being in daily life. *Journal of Personality and Social Psychology, 84,* 377–389.

Enright, R. D. (2001). *Forgiveness is a choice: A step-by-step process for resolving anger and restoring hope.* Washington, DC: American Psychological Association.

Erikson, E. H., Erikson, J. M., & Kivnick, H. Q. (1986). *Vital involvement in old age.* New York: W. W. Norton.

Fact Monster (2000–2007). De Kooning, Willem. *http://www.factmonster. com/ce6/.html.* The Columbia Electronic Encyclopedia. Pearson Education, publishing as Fact Monster.

Findsen, B. (2005). *Learning later.* Malbar, FL: Kieger.

Fitzgerald, P. (1998). Gratitude and justice. *Ethics, 109,* 119–153.

Gawande, L. (2007, March 14). The way we age now. *New Yorker*, 51–58.

Griswald, C. (2007). *Forgiveness: A philosophical exploration*. New York: Cambridge University Press.

Gross, J. (2007). Divorced, Middle-Aged and Happy: Women, especially adjust to the 90's. *New York Times*, December 17, 1992.

Hamerman, D. (1999). Toward an understanding of frailty. *Annals of Internal Medicine, 130(11)*, 945–950.

Harris, A. H. S., & Thoresen, C. E. (2005). Volunteering is associated with delayed mortality in older people: Analysis of the longitudinal study of aging. *Journal of Health Psychology, 10(6)*, 739–752.

Hill, R. D. (2005). *Positive aging: A guide for mental health professionals and consumers*. New York: W. W. Norton.

Hill, R. D., & Gregg, C. (2002). Older adults in residential care: A population at risk. In R. D. Hill, B. Thorn, J. Bowling, & T. Morrison (Eds.), *Geriatric residential care*. Mahaw, NJ: Erlbaum.

Hill, R. D., & Mansour, E. (2008). The role of positive aging in addressing the mental health needs of older adults. In L. Thompson and D. Gallagher (Eds.), *Handbook of behavioral and cognitive strategies therapies with older adults*. Springer: New York.

Hultsch, D. J., Hertzog, C., Small, B. J., & Dixon, R. A. (1999). Use it or lose it: Engaged lifestyle as a buffer of cognitive decline in aging. *Psychology and Aging, 14*, 245–263.

Ingersoll-Dayton, B., & Krause, N. (2005). Self-forgiveness: A component of mental health in later life. *Research on Aging, 27*, 267–289.

Jung, C. G. (1984). *Modern man in search of a soul*. New York: Routledge.

Komter, A. E. (2004). Gratitude and gift exchange. In R. A. Emmons & M. E. McCullough (Eds.), *The psychology of gratitude*, pp. 195–212. New York: Oxford University Press.

Kushner, H. (1994). *When bad things happen to good people*. New York: Simon & Schuster.

Lawler, K. A., Younger, J. W., Piferi, R. L., Jobe, R. L., Edmundson, K. A., & Jones, W. H. (2005). The unique effects of forgiveness on health: An exploration of pathways. *Journal of Behavioral Medicine, 28*, 157–167.

Lerner, R. M. (1986). *Concepts and theories of human development* (2nd ed.). New York: Random House.

Lockenhoff, C. E., & Carstensen, L. L. (2004). Socioemotional selectivity theory, aging, and health: The increasingly delicate balance between regulating emotions and making tough choices. *Journal of Personality, 72*, 68–78.

Luskin, F. (2003). *Forgive for good: A proven prescription for health and happiness*. New York: HarperCollins.

Maltby, J., Day, L., & Barber, L. (2004). Forgiveness and mental health variables: Interpreting the relationship using an adaptational-continuum

model of personality and coping. *Personality and Individual Differences,*
37, 1629–1641.

Manning, A. (2005). Aging divinely is a concern. *USA Today,* p. A3.

Millman, L. (1987). *A kayak full of ghosts: Eskimo tales.* Santa Barbara, CA:
Capra Press.

Morrow-Howell, N., Hinterlong, J., Rozario, P. A., & Tang, F. (2003).
Effects of volunteering on the well-being of older adults. *Journal of
Gerontology Series B: Psychological Sciences and Social Sciences, 58,*
S137–S145.

Neff, K. D. (2003). Self-compassion: An alternative conceptualization of
a healthy attitude towards oneself. *Self and Identity, 2,* 85–102.

Newberg, A. B., d'Aquili, E. G., Newberg, S. K., & deMarici, V. (2000).
The neuropsychological correlates of forgiveness. In M. McCullough,
K. I. Pargament, C. Thoresen (Eds.), *Forgiveness: Theory, research, and
practice.* New York: Guilford Press.

Ong, A. D., Bergeman, C. S., & Bisconti, T. L. (2004). The role of daily
emotions during conjugal bereavement. *Journal of Gerontology:
Psychological Sciences, 59,* 168–176.

Park, D. C., Gutchess, A. H., Meade, M. L., & Stine-Morrow, A. L.
(2007). Improving cognitive function in older adults: Nontraditional approaches. *Journals of Gerontology Series B: Psychological Sciences and Social
Sciences, 62,* 45–52.

Park, N., Peterson, C., & Seligman, M. E. P. (2005). Orientations to happiness and life satisfaction: The full versus the empty life. *Journal of
Happiness Studies, 6(1),* 25–41.

Penner, L. A. (2002). The causes of sustained volunteerism: An interac-
tionist perspective. *Journal of Social Issues, 58,* 447–467.

Roberts, R. C. (2004). The blessings of gratitude: A conceptual analysis.
In R. A. Emmons & M. E. McCullough, (Eds.), *The psychology of gratitude,* pp. 195–212. New York: Oxford University Press.

Rodin, J., & Langer, E. (1977). Long-term effect of a control-relevant
intervention. *Journal of Personality & Social Psychology, 36,* 12–29.

Seligman, M. E. P., & Csikszentmihalyi, M. (2000). Positive psychology:
An introduction. *American Psychologist, 55,* 5–14.

Shinn, M., & Toohey, S. M. (2003). Community contexts of human welfare. *Annual Review of Psychology, 54,* 427–459.

Shock, N. W., Greulich, R. C., Costas Jr., P. T., Andres, R., Iakatta, E. G.,
Arenberg, D., et al. (1984). Normal human aging: The Baltimore Longitudinal Study of Aging. Washington, DC: National Institutes of Health.

Singh, P. (2007). Altruism, The essence of all knowledge. from http://
spirituality.indiatimes.com/cms.dll/articleshow?ArticleID=407696078.

Soka-Gakkai. (2007). The four virtues of the living buddha. *Living
Buddhism,* Volume, 8 DOI: http://www.sgi-usa.org/buddhism/bud-
dhismtoday/.

Stevens, N. L., Martina, C. M. S., & Westerhof, G. J. (2006). Meeting the need to belong: Predicting effects of a friendship enrichment program for older women. *Gerontologist, 46(4),* 495–502.

Stroebe, M. S., Hansson, R. O., Stroebe, W., & Henk, S. (2001). *Handbook of bereavement research: Consequences, coping, and care.* Washington, DC: American Psychological Association.

Thoresen, C. E., Harris, A. H. S., & Luskin, F. (2000). Forgiveness and health: An unanswered question. In M. E. McCollough, K. I. Pargament, & C. E. Thoresen (Eds.), *Forgiveness: Theory, research, and practice,* pp. 245–280. New York: Guilford Press.

Thorn, B. (2002). Defining residential care from a developmental perspective. In R. D. Hill, B. Thorn, J. Bowling, & T. Morrison (Eds.), *Geriatric Residential Care,* pp. 21–38. Mahwah, NJ: Erlbaum.

Transcredi, L. (2005). *Hardwired behavior: What neuroscience reveals about morality.* New York: Cambridge University Press.

Twain, M. (1981). *The Adventures of Tom Sawyer.* Chicago, IL: The John Winston Co.

U.S. Bureau of Labor Statistics. (2006). Volunteering in the United States, 2006. U.S. Bureau of Labor Statistics, Division of Labor Force Statistics. USDL 07-0019.

U.S. Bureau of Labor Statistics. (2007). Volunteering in the United States 2006. USDL 07-0019. January 17. http://www.bls.gov/cps/.

Valliant, G. E. (2002). *Aging well: Surprising guideposts to a happier life.* Boston: Little, Brown.

Verbrugge, L. M., & Jette, A. M. (1994). The disablement process. *Social Science Medicine, 38,* 1–14.

West, J. O. (1988). *Mexican-American folklore: Legends, songs, festivals, proverbs, crafts, tales of saints, of revolutionaries, and more.* Little Rock, AR: August House.

Wilson, R. S., Mendes de Leon, C. F., Barnes, L. L., Schneider, J. A., Bienias, J. L., Evans, D. A., et al. (2002). Participation in cognitively stimulating activities and risk of incident Alzheimer disease. *Journal of the American Medical Association, 287,* 742–748.

INDEX